BLOODY NASTY PEOPLE
The Rise of Britain's Far Right

by
DANIEL TRILLING

VERSO
London • New York

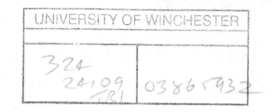
This revised paperback edition first published by Verso 2013
First published by Verso 2012
© Daniel Trilling 2012, 2013

1 3 5 7 9 10 8 6 4 2

Verso
UK: 6 Meard Street, London W1F 0EG
US: 20 Jay Street, Suite 1010, Brooklyn, NY 11201

www.versobooks.com

Verso is the imprint of New Left Books

ISBN-13: 978-1-78168-080-3

British Library Cataloguing in Publication Data
A catalogue record for this book is available from the British Library

Library of Congress Cataloging-in-Publication Data
The Library of Congress has cataloged the hardcover edition as follows:
Trilling, Daniel.
Bloody nasty people : the rise of Britain's far right / by Daniel Trilling.
p. cm.
Includes bibliographical references and index.
ISBN 978-1-84467-959-1 (hardback : alk. paper) – ISBN 978-1-84467-960-7 (ebook)
1. British National Party (1982–) I. Title.
JN1129.B75T75 2012
324.241'093–dc23
2012022591

Typeset in Fournier by Hewer Text UK, ltd, Edinburgh
Printed and bound in the UK by
CPI Group (UK) Ltd, Croydon, CR0 4YY

Contents

Introduction

On a spring afternoon in early 2011, I was sitting outside a country pub, when a car pulled up. Out stepped two well-built minders, followed by the portly figure of Nick Griffin, chairman of the British National Party. The BNP has the dubious distinction of being Britain's most successful far-right party ever; despite roots in a neo-Nazi subculture, it notched up a string of victories in local elections over the past decade, along with two seats in the European Parliament, before an electoral collapse in 2010. It remains an ugly presence on the country's political landscape, with Griffin periodically invited onto national media to promote the BNP's racist policies. Yet, for all that, it has been little understood.

I was hoping to find out more. Griffin could not meet me in central London – a 'security risk', he had told me when we spoke on the phone – so instead we had arranged to meet here, a few miles outside the Essex town of Epping. ('Are you a real ale drinker?' he had asked me. 'Choose a pub from the *Good Beer Guide.*') The trio looked tired and grumpy when they emerged from the car. Because he is so widely despised, Griffin can't take public transport and so spends hours crammed alongside his hired muscle into a grey hatchback. He speaks ever so slightly too fast, like a man who is used to being heckled or cut off mid-sentence. Since he was elected to the European Parliament in 2009 this semi-fugitive lifestyle has intensified as he makes regular trips across France and Belgium. Griffin, dressed in a dark suit, walked over, shook my hand and sat down; one of his minders nipped inside the pub and returned carrying an unappetizing on-the-road snack: half a Cornish pasty, on a paper napkin, and a packet of dry-roasted peanuts. 'This is lunch, that's why I'm not sharing any with you,' Griffin said, mouth full, as I fiddled with my Dictaphone and searched in my bag for a notebook.

'So,' Griffin eventually said, brushing peanut dust from his jacket sleeves. 'Tell me about this book.'

In April 2008, the *New Statesman* sent me to review a music festival in East London's Victoria Park, held to mark the thirtieth anniversary of Rock Against Racism, the cultural movement that had galvanized opposition to the National Front in the late 1970s. My parents, both of whom had gone on antiracist demos during this period, had told me stories about Rock Against Racism when I was younger, and I was excited to see some of that spirit revisited. It was timely, too: for several years, the British National Party had been growing in prominence, winning seats on a number of councils across England. Elections to the London Assembly, where the BNP was expected to pick up support, were only a few days away.

But something seemed wrong: while thousands of smiling, ethnically diverse teenagers turned out to see the bands, under the slogan 'love music, hate racism', it felt strangely detached from reality. Thirty years previously, Victoria Park, in the heart of London's East End, had been the front line of the fight against the National Front. In 2008, the BNP was gaining support on the outskirts of the capital, miles away from cosmopolitan inner London. The image of its supporters was not that of angry young skinheads, but of pessimistic ex-Labour voters. And surely Britain, too, was a changed place? Hadn't the battle by black and Asian immigrants to have equal place in popular culture been won? Hate racism? Well, of course – nobody in twenty-first-century Britain wanted to be known as a *racist*, not even the BNP.

At the time, I could not articulate these thoughts, and my overly cynical review of the festival drew stinging criticism from trade union leaders who had helped organize the event. Praise came from one quarter only: a BNP website that crowed about the party's seemingly unstoppable rise. A few days later, the BNP candidate Richard Barnbrook was elected to the London Assembly with over 5 per cent of the vote. A relatively small achievement, but another first for a party whose opponents were adamant was a fascist one. 'Knocking on doors is the secret of our success,' claimed the website, adding: 'Our strategy of meeting voters face to face on the doorstep and backing up our campaigns with well produced and easy-to-read election leaflets is providing the right results. There has been much talk . . . of the Labour Party being disengaged from voters – and it is. The BNP on the other hand, through our canvassing, are fully connected.'

'Fully connected'? What on earth did that mean? And how exactly did a party whose own constitution bore a commitment to 'reversing the tide of non-white immigration and to restoring . . . the overwhelmingly white makeup of the British population that existed in Britain prior to 1948' win votes simply by 'knocking on doors'?

These questions, and more, led me to think about this book. Who are the 'bloody nasty people' to whom the title refers? Most obvious are the men (and a few women) who have devoted their lives to fascist and racist politics. They are not foaming-at-the-mouth monsters – indeed, to be so would require far too unstable a temperament for the painstaking and unglamorous work they have put in, over years and decades, towards making the BNP a successful political party. Some may be oddballs and loners; others may be loving parents and partners; and many are gregarious (among the right people, of course). Like most of us, members of the BNP will be a combination of all these things. But they have committed themselves to a politics that even in its 'voter-friendly' incarnation would cause untold misery and conflict among the people of this country.

But there is a distinction between committed BNP members and those who have been drawn to support the party. Most – numbering well over a million – will have voted BNP at some point in the past decade. Some will have leafleted or canvassed. A few have even stood for election. There is a persistent image of these people as dejected, racist 'white working class'. This has been distorted because the image of BNP voters is a powerful tool politically. In some quarters the accusation of bigotry has been a convenient way to dismiss legitimate concerns over jobs and housing. In others, such people have been evoked piously by advocates of a halt to immigration, or by those who proclaim the death of multiculturalism. We will see how this fits into a wider problem Britain has with addressing class, where working-class people have been virtually banished from our politics and media, only to return sentimentalized or demonized according to the occasion. 'Bloody nasty people' was a 2004 headline taken from the *Sun* – and I have used it to raise a question: to what extent have the actions of established politicians, and the mainstream media, given the BNP fertile ground on which to operate? And do the same factors lie behind the more recent emergence of the English Defence League?

Fascism is a heavily contested term: to use it will immediately conjure up images of Hitler and swastikas, or of Mussolini and jackboots. To many people it denotes a particular style of authoritarian politics, located in a historical era that has now passed, and may seem an unhelpful term when discussing the BNP and English Defence League.

For the purposes of this book, I have taken the work of the American historian Robert O. Paxton as my guide. In *The Anatomy of Fascism*, Paxton explains that while fascist movements throughout the modern period have varied in appearance and tactics, they 'resemble each other mainly in their functions'. In other words, fascism is not a question of what clothes you wear or what poses you adopt. Rather, as Paxton attempts to define it, 'fascism is a system of political authority and social order intended to reinforce the unity, energy and purity of communities in which liberal democracy stands accused of producing division and decline.'

This may sound vague at first, but this is because fascism does not offer a fixed set of policies; rather it seeks to recruit followers and bind them around a pole of extreme nationalism by appealing to what Paxton terms as 'mobilising passions': fear, betrayal, resentment, a mortal enemy within or without. 'Feelings,' he writes, 'propel fascism more than thought does.' Those 'passions' – the raw material of fascism – are not the preserve of a small group of fanatics, but exist in society at large.

In general, however, I have opted to use the more neutral term 'far right' when referring to the BNP and EDL. This

covers a range of political positions, from anti-immigrant populism to outright fascism. It will become clear over the course of
my argument that the BNP is fascist in origin, and has remained
so at heart – but it has been able to progress only by appealing
to a wider set of far-right interests. The EDL is an even looser
grouping. I use the term 'neo-Nazi' only to refer to groups or
individuals who seek to recreate the policies, or adopt the visual
symbols, of the German Nazi Party. In the BNP's history, there
have been more than a few.

In Britain, the far right has often been portrayed as an aberration, a foreign malady imported into an otherwise tolerant
milieu. This has had great strategic value for its opponents:
highlighting the Hitler-worshipping tendencies of the National
Front's leaders during the 1970s was an easy way to discredit a
supposedly patriotic movement. But this risks obscuring the
home-grown intellectual traditions on which parties like the
BNP draw. And by regarding them in isolation, we can also
miss what they share in common with the political mainstream,
the sources from which their propaganda draws its appeal.

As Enoch Powell once remarked, 'The life of nations . . . is
lived largely in the imagination.' If that is so, then the story of
the BNP takes us into the darker corners of this national fantasy.
It may force us to confront some unpleasant truths about
Britain, but it is vital we overcome our revulsion and examine it
carefully: we must peer into its eyes, even if we risk finding
ourselves reflected back.

It was getting dark in Essex, so Griffin and I moved inside the
pub. Towards the end of our interview, during which the pub
had been empty, a couple of men in rugby shirts came in and sat
by the bar. After Griffin left (I thanked him politely and told

him I hope he never succeeds), one of the men called over: 'Good luck with the interview.' Easy to spot I'm a journalist, I suppose. I apologized for having brought Griffin into their pub and explained that he wouldn't meet me in central London.

'Fine by me, mate,' said one in a confident leer. I was puzzled by the ambiguity of that statement – was he happy for his local to be used by journalists? Or was the interviewee more welcome than the interviewer? I didn't stick around to find out more. I stepped out of the pub with the questions left hanging.

PART I

1

A Nasty Little Local Difficulty

The Island is a funny place. People fall out with people, some groups fall out with one another. But if someone's back is against the wall, they'll all stand together. Because otherwise, they'll pick you off one by one.

Rita Bensley, Association of Island Communities

The night of 16 September 1993 provided an unpleasant moment of farce to punctuate a slow, grinding tragedy. As protestors from the Anti-Nazi League gathered outside the Isle of Dogs neighbourhood centre, officials from Tower Hamlets Council were sifting through ballots cast in a local by-election. At 10.30 p.m., a murmur of surprise ran through the room as the Labour candidate, James Hunt, asked for a recount. He should have walked this election. Now, visibly shaken, Hunt wasn't so sure of himself. Just before eleven, an eighty-strong mob of skinheads emerged from nearby pubs and headed for the crowd outside the centre, chorusing 'Rule Britannia'. One threw a milk bottle, which smashed among his opponents. As police broke up the ensuing scuffles, inside the building the election result was quietly confirmed. Derek Beackon, an unemployed van driver and candidate for the

British National Party, had won the Millwall by-election by just seven votes.

It may have only been one local council seat out of thousands – and two fewer than were held at the time by the Monster Raving Loony Party – but the election of a BNP candidate sent ripples far beyond the Isle of Dogs. Over the days that followed, news crews and reporters descended on this little spit of land that sticks out into the Thames from London's East End. They wanted to know why 1,480 of its residents had voted for a man with a twenty-year history of involvement in racist street politics, whose campaign leaflets complained that 'our children are being forced to learn the languages and religions and cultures of Asia, forced to eat their food', demanded 'Rights for Whites' and promised to 'put the British people first'.

Was this an aberration, 'a nasty little local difficulty', as the *Daily Mail* put it? Academics were wheeled out to explain the East End's association with far-right movements, stretching back almost a century, via the National Front and Sir Oswald Mosley's Blackshirts, to the British Brothers' League of 1902. This part of London had for centuries been a stopping-off point for immigrants, something that had long made it a target for demagogues seeking to whip up hatred. Now, just as newspapers were reporting preparations for the fiftieth anniversary of Hitler's defeat, voters in one of the areas hit hardest by the Blitz had delivered a stinging rebuke to the establishment by electing a fascist.

And perhaps there was more to come. 'The people of East London have always been known for their tolerance and easygoing temperament. Recently some of them, and there are many more, have got fed up with being undermined,' warned one letter-writer to the local paper. 'They voted for the one who had the guts to speak on their behalf.'[1]

What, though, was being undermined?

'I was the last registered stevedore in Millwall Dock,' George Pye told me, as we sat in his office at St John's Community Centre, a small room dominated by a painting in which a square-jawed docker thrust a piece of paper under the nose of his cowering boss. 'When they closed the dock – or murdered it, I should say – I was on holiday. All the other dockers went to Tilbury but when I came back, I refused.'

Pye, a fifth generation 'Islander', as many locals here refer to themselves, was describing the devastation visited upon his neighbourhood when the docks that had sustained it closed in 1980. 'When we opened this place [in the early 1980s], it was packed. You used to get lots of families down here because you could bring your kids. Now the only ones left are pockets of older people.' It was a Friday night, but the streets outside were almost deserted, and the centre's function room was nearly empty, with only a handful of elderly white men and women drinking and playing darts. Were it not for the towers of Canary Wharf that loomed nearby, you might never have guessed that this place had been at the crossroads of an empire for more than two centuries – or that Pye's story was proof of the destruction it could leave in its wake.

Lying just a couple of miles from the City, the Isle of Dogs, a marshy peninsula surrounded by water on three sides, was transformed into a hub of international trade with the opening of the West India Dock in 1802. As Britain's empire grew, so did the docks, and migrants from Britain, Ireland and Europe were drawn to work there, their fortunes tied to the booms and slumps of the global economy. Slum conditions and precarious employment led to the formation of the modern trade union movement at the end of the nineteenth century – and a tradition of protest that is still celebrated in East End legend. The 'Island' was severely damaged by the Luftwaffe during the Second World War, but those inhabitants who stayed were rewarded with a huge programme of council house building.

When the London docks began a slow but steady decline after the Second World War, hit by a fall in manufacturing exports and the rise of containerization, the East End was bereft. In 1955, they had given work to 31,000 people – by 1975, this had fallen to 9,800. And the industries that supported shipping were cut adrift, too: 75,000 jobs were lost in East London between 1971 and 1981.[2] Islanders, cut off from the rest of the East End (literally so, when the swing bridges at the north end of the peninsula were raised to let ships pass) were particularly hard hit, voicing their discontent in 1970 when a group of local campaigners issued a 'Unilateral Declaration of Independence'.

The final blow was delivered by the Thatcher Government in 1980 – a move that Pye, like many of his colleagues, saw as political. 'It was like with the miners, Maggie took the unions on in stages.' Pye was hardly a militant – he told me, proudly, that his union branch had only ever gone on strike twice in three decades – but even today, he is adamant that the docks could have been saved. 'What makes me so bitter is that all this time, they were saying, "We need to move into the twenty-first century." Well we had containerization here, we had a bigger berth for the bigger ships, we had cruise ships docking here. The apple and pear trade from New Zealand and Australia was guaranteed for another three years. Everything they was talking about we were doing.'

Instead, the government's solution was a combination of top-down diktat and economic laissez-faire – the essence, perhaps, of what became Thatcherism. In 1981, the London Docklands Development Corporation (LDDC) was established as a private company; the following year, a huge swathe of London's riverside, stretching east along the Thames Estuary was designated an Enterprise Zone, offering low tax rates and lax planning regulations to property developers. The idea was to transform Docklands, as it was rebranded, into a world financial centre, focused on Canary Wharf. Former dock land was sold off for development, prompting land values to soar; a new gold rush from which the Islanders were excluded. Despite £6 billion of public money being spent on 'regeneration', unemployment remained 20 per cent on the Isle of Dogs. 'There was a missed opportunity here,' said Pye, who today works as a pierman, unloading boatloads of tourists and City workers at Canary Wharf. 'The finance stuff is fine, but they put all their eggs in one basket. It's crazy not to use water when you've got the Thames on your doorstep.'

Islanders were furious: they were watching steel and glass palaces rise in front of them, yet their children couldn't find jobs or, increasingly, a place to live. The Right to Buy scheme – a Thatcher Government policy introduced in 1980 that gave council tenants the right to buy their homes at subsidised rates – was eating away at the number of council homes available, and the LDDC was actively hostile to building more social housing, preferring to encourage developments aimed at affluent professionals. In July 1986, protesters from the Association of Island Communities released thousands of bees and a flock of sheep into a tent where the cream of the world's finance industry had gathered to watch the governor of the Bank of

England turn the first sod of earth to mark the beginning of construction work at Canary Wharf.[3] Beyond a few colourful headlines, their protest was ignored.

One year later, a new dimension would be added to this already fractious situation. My conversation with Pye took a pause, as he attended to two Asian women in headscarves who had come to book the function room for a wedding. 'I'll give you a discount, as you won't be needing the bar, I take it?'

In 1987, sixteen-year-old Syeda Choudhury, along with her parents, brother and sister, became one of the first Bengali families to move on to the Isle of Dogs. 'It was scary,' Choudhury told me, her accent a mix of Cockney and Bengali, when we met in 2011. 'We lived up by Commercial Road [in Whitechapel, north-west of the Isle of Dogs], where lots of other Bengalis lived. A lot of people had told us that the Isle of Dogs was not a nice area, but at that time the council made only one offer for housing, so you had to take what you could get.' The Choudhurys took up residence on the Barkantine estate, whose pointy-roofed tower blocks still stand today, a stubborn objection to the skyscrapers of Canary Wharf. The 'Islanders' were never a homogenous community; estates like Barkantine had long been used to house tenants from elsewhere in London. But in the past they had been white. 'We were the only Bengali people in our block – and in the two or three other blocks, there was like one or two families.' The Choudhurys soon found they were not welcome.

East London's Bengalis, their lives marked by the same empire that had sustained the docks, were no strangers to hostility: the thousands of families like the Choudhurys who had arrived from Bangladesh during the 1960s and 1970s had faced abuse and systematic discrimination since their arrival. Asian families were far more likely to experience homelessness or overcrowded living conditions,[4] and had been a target for violence encouraged by the BNP's forerunner, the National Front, during the 1970s and 80s. Choudhury remembers her shock the first time she saw a gang of Union Jack-toting racists: 'I was nine when we came over from Bangladesh and we used to love this Union Jack, everyone loves the British Queen. But when I saw it here, in their hands, and the way they were abusing it, you don't like it any more.'

By the mid-80s, Bengalis had resisted the worst racism, but in 1987, the Choudhurys were dropped into the middle of an acute housing crisis. As the Island's waterfront properties had been sold off for private development, the Right to Buy scheme was severely diminishing the available housing stock: in 1985 there were 5,537 council homes on the Isle of Dogs; by 1993 this had fallen to 4,000.[5] Community life on the Isle of Dogs had already been torn asunder when many dockers moved downriver to work at the Tilbury container port; now the remaining working-class residents found it increasingly difficult to ensure that their friends and relatives were housed nearby.

This problem was by no means confined to the Island – across Tower Hamlets, one of the country's poorest boroughs, housing was in short supply. A shortage of homes, combined with rising unemployment, had bred discontent at the borough's long-reigning Labour administration, and in 1986 Tower Hamlets elected a Liberal-run council. The Liberals (who became the Liberal Democrats in 1988) had won power with a populist campaign that sought to play up fears of crime and social breakdown and promised a 'Sons and Daughters' housing scheme, which would ensure 'local' people were at the front of the queue for homes.

This was an empty promise, since councils were obliged by law to house homeless families first. What's more, as the Liberals were well aware, to many East Londoners 'local' meant 'white'. Once in power, councillors sought to shore up their position by playing on white resentment. In 1987, Liberal councillors claimed that Bengali families living in bed and breakfast accommodation had made themselves intentionally homeless by coming to Britain; a year later, the mayor of Tower Hamlets, Jeremy Shaw, staged a publicity stunt, willingly relayed by the *East London Advertiser*, when he travelled to Bangladesh to tell the government there that Tower Hamlets had no more room for migrants.[6]

And while the Liberals raised the hopes of white Tower Hamlets residents, their commitment to localism had created a further problem: power in the borough was devolved into 'neighbourhoods', each with their own budget and spending powers. The Isle of Dogs neighbourhood was represented by three Labour councillors and when Asian families began arriving in 1987, many white residents blamed Labour for giving away homes they believed should have been theirs. As Pye, who stood as a Lib Dem council candidate in 1990, put it to me: 'Everybody felt that Labour was fine on the Bengalis or West Indians or whatever, but if you were white you got nothing. The feeling was, we've got to get houses, same as anybody else.'

Pye is no bigot, and he has worked hard to make people of the different colours and creeds who inhabit the Isle of Dogs today feel welcome: St John's provides space for Muslim prayer sessions, plus West Indian, African and Anglican church congregations. But during the late 80s, other Islanders let their resentment spill over into something much nastier. Choudhury recalled being chased off a bus by white youths shortly after moving to the Isle of Dogs ('I ran home and just shut the curtains'), and described a steadily worsening atmosphere as more Asian families moved onto the Island. 'You couldn't go to the park, never. If I went to the park, to play, on the swings and stuff, there would be white boys and girls chasing me. They used to bring dogs to chase you. We had to come home before dark, much earlier than other people. In winter you had to get home as soon as it turned four o'clock.'

Between 1987 and 1988, 104 racist attacks were reported to the Isle of Dogs housing office, despite only 260 Bangladeshi families living on the Island at the time. The next year, the number of incidents doubled, leaving people terrified. On one estate, some Bengali women had not been out of their home for more than six months.[7] 'If you're not Bengali, Asian, you'd think "oh, come on"; you wouldn't believe it,' Choudhury insists. 'But that was the reality. It happened.'

A photo of Eddy Butler from the early 1990s reveals a gaunt young man in a black bomber jacket, leading members of the BNP's feared 'security' team Combat 18[8] through the streets of London's East End. Butler's determined stare suggests that he relishes what he described to me, in retrospect, as the 'high adrenaline' pursuits of the BNP.[9] Formed in 1982, after a split in the National Front, the BNP was led by John Tyndall, a neo-Nazi with a long pedigree in the most extreme and violent quarters of Britain's far right. Its political programme demanded the forcible 'repatriation' of non-white Britons, and proposed the restoration of the British Empire along with a series of authoritarian measures derived from Hitler. The

BNP followed a familiar pattern of holding provocative marches and rallies; its members attacked left-wing meetings and sought to create ethnic divisions by encouraging – or even perpetrating – racist assaults.[10]

Butler, a former National Front member, had joined the party in 1986 and before long was given the position of East London organizer. By the early 90s, the BNP was gaining notoriety thanks to a string of racist murders near its south-east London headquarters in Welling – which culminated in the killing of a black teenager, Stephen Lawrence, in 1993 – and by launching a 'Rights for Whites' campaign in Tower Hamlets, overseen by Butler.[11] 'Rights for Whites' was a slogan used in 1990 after the stabbing of a white teenager by his Asian classmates. The boy's parents had complained that police were not taking the crime seriously and the BNP hijacked their campaign, holding rallies and public meetings in the Bethnal Green area.

Not since the days of the National Front had there been such a concerted effort by the far right to spark conflict in the East End. But the Rights for Whites marches marked a departure for the BNP, who had been inspired by the success of the Lib Dems' 'community politics' strategy. As Butler put it, 'Instead of focusing on national issues and complex aspects of party policy, we simply appealed to ordinary whites . . . by discussing the local issues that concerned and worried them.'[12] For the far right, local and national elections had long been used as a way to gain publicity, mainly by holding election 'meetings' that would inevitably turn violent. But the Rights for Whites strategy also began to pay dividends in local elections, enticing 'patriotically inclined' voters away from the Lib Dems, who in the eyes of the BNP 'had been perceived as a party that at local level defended white interests'.[13] At a 1990 by-election in

Bethnal Green, the BNP candidate helped overturn a Lib Dem majority of 800, handing the seat to Labour.

After 1992, the BNP began to abandon the public meetings and take electioneering more seriously. Partly this was a result of necessity: Squads of militant anti-fascists had literally beaten BNP activists off the streets,[14] but activists like Butler also thought the party had a real chance of winning seats. The tactics, as he explained, were primitive to begin with: 'We had a series of by-elections where we were improving our tactics, copying what the Liberal Democrats did, doing very simple leaflets on local issues. Each time we were improving our canvassing techniques, doing multiple sweeps. We didn't use canvass sheets at first, we'd just use the electoral register and draw lines down. It's a mathematical thing; if you identify people then you've got people to get out on polling day. The more you knock, the more people you find. For a party like us, explaining to people on the door why they should vote for us is more important than for other parties.'

These efforts focused largely on Bethnal Green and Bow, districts at the north end of Tower Hamlets, but the 1992 general election delivered a surprise: With hardly any canvassing, there had been a surge of support for the BNP to the south, on the Isle of Dogs.

Since the Choudhurys had moved on to the Island in 1987 hostility towards Bengalis had continued to rise, as demand for housing grew ever tighter. The construction of a tunnel to bring traffic into Canary Wharf – the Limehouse Link, still the most expensive road scheme in Britain per mile – meant that several blocks of council flats had to be demolished and their largely Asian residents rehoused. Things came to a head in early 1992, over the first social housing scheme in a decade to be built on the Isle of Dogs. In January, a group of Island residents proposed that all properties on Masthouse Terrace, a riverside development of homes ranging from one-bedroom flats to eight-bedroom houses, be allocated to 'Islanders' only, and that a ban be imposed on housing homeless people from outside the area.[15] Then a local newspaper article claimed, erroneously, that twenty-one out of the development's twenty-five homes had been allocated to Bengali families, with some receiving £5,000 to buy furniture.[16] Finally, some new housing was being built – and it all appeared to be going to Asians. The Labour-run neighbourhood was powerless to intervene – housing was being allocated on the basis of need, in line with the law – and the Lib Dem council had broken its promise to provide homes for 'Sons and Daughters'.

At a by-election in October 1992, the BNP came third in Millwall, with 20 per cent of the vote. Immediately after, the BNP distributed a 'well done' leaflet to homes on the Isle of Dogs that described the 20 per cent vote as 'a well-deserved kick in the pants for the old complacent parties. But we'd have done even better if some of you had not lost your bottle or stayed at home.'[17] Activists began to visit Millwall on a regular basis, selling the party paper and following up membership enquiries. Several months later, another by-election was announced, to be held in October 1993. Derek Beackon, the BNP's chief steward, offered to stand. As Butler explained, the BNP was well-placed to pick up on local resentment: 'We had our ear to the ground, so we knew what was going on. I used to live on the Isle of Dogs at one point and I knew the area. Derek Beackon's sister lived on the Isle of Dogs. My partner's brother lived on the Isle of Dogs. People knew people who would know what was going on in the estates. So you could do leaflets in tune with what people were talking about.'

As campaigning intensified, the Lib Dems redoubled their own efforts, distributing an 'Island Homes for Island People' newsletter, which demanded that Labour councillors 'listen to Islanders and not the Commission for Racial Equality'.[18] The Lib Dems also toured the constituency in cars flying Union Jacks and tried to paint their Labour rivals as unfairly favoring Bengali residents, distributing a leaflet that claimed Millwall councillors had given £30,000 to Bangladesh for flood relief rather than spending it on local repairs.[19]

All the while, the luxury apartments and office blocks continued to rise, on land that had once provided working-class jobs. The connection seems so obvious in retrospect – but the inhabitants of 'yuppie' flats, in gated developments and driving on and off the Island by way of the Limehouse Link, were in another world. As Sheila, a white resident of the Barkantine estate (where the Choudhurys also lived) told me, 'None of the yuppies ever bothered us. At least you knew they were paying their way. That's what you wanted.'

Then, one week before the 1993 by-election, Labour made a disastrous error. On 9 September, in an effort to squeeze the Lib Dems out of the race, Labour leaked a canvass report that claimed it was neck and neck with the BNP, on 34 per cent each.[20] The idea was to scare voters into supporting Labour – but it also worked in reverse. As John Biggs, a former Tower Hamlets Labour councillor (and now London Assembly member), explains, while Tower Hamlets at the time was run by Liberal Democrats, many ordinary residents would still have perceived Labour, which had dominated local politics for decades, as the 'establishment': 'People don't sit at home going through the last opinion polls and the last election results and say "ah, it's the Liberal council". They blamed Labour for the state of housing on the Isle of Dogs and they wanted to work out who best to vote for to give Labour a kicking.'

It may only have been on a small scale, but this was a total breakdown of mainstream politics: the Isle of Dogs was a Labour-run neighbourhood, in a Lib Dem-run borough, under a Tory Government – and nobody seemed able to provide the basic necessities. As one Island resident, Maureen Lowther, 49, told the *East London Advertiser* several days after Beackon's election: 'It's not a racial thing, it's resentment. You are getting Bangladeshis getting eight-bedroom houses. Of course we're going to be resentful. I'm not in full agreement with all the BNP stands for, but Rights for Whites, yes. All them councillors have created this situation, they are fighting against racism but why aren't they fighting for all? All we want is equality.'[21]

On the Sunday after Derek Beackon's election, the Reverend Nicholas Holtam gave a sheet of paper to his congregation at Christ Church on the Isle of Dogs and asked them to write down how they felt. The page was soon filled with words like 'angry', 'tearful', 'ashamed', 'frightened' and 'pissed off'. One elderly man, a member of the British Legion, left the church in tears. 'I spent four years of my life fighting Nazis, and now we've voted them in,' he told Holtam as he walked out.[22]

With 33.8 per cent of the vote, the BNP never represented the majority of Islanders, and many whites had bitterly opposed the party. The day after the election, unionised council workers on the Isle of Dogs went on strike in protest at Beackon's election (the first of a series of walk-outs), and groups including the Anti-Nazi League, the Anti-Racist Alliance and Youth Against

Racism in Europe continued to organize protests across Tower Hamlets. Large anti-racism demos were also held in Trafalgar Square and at the BNP's headquarters in Welling.

As Holtam – who is now the Bishop of Salisbury – told me when we met in 2011, the country's media now seemed to regard the BNP as an expression of white working-class East Enders' inherent stupidity and bigotry, seemingly encapsulated by the 'Cockney Wanker' character in the satirical magazine *Viz* shortly after Beackon's victory. 'There were jokes on TV about Millwall and the Isle of Dogs,' Holtam continued. 'The rest of the country looked at us and laughed. It was a hideous time.'

But the problems thrown into sharp relief by Beackon's victory were national as much as they were local. Britain in 1993 was in the grip of an economic recession and John Major, derided by the *Telegraph* as 'the least popular leader since polls began', had taken to peddling sentimental nostalgia in speeches evoking a bygone England of warm beer and village greens. One of his backbench MPs, Winston Churchill (a grandson of the former prime minister), went further, warning that summer that the 'British way of life' itself was under threat from immigration. On 20 September, Churchill prophesied more fascist victories in British cities unless the government cracked down on immigration.[23]

On 26 September, the *News of the World* risked further inflaming the situation in Tower Hamlets by sending one white and one Asian journalist to the council's housing office. The two did not present identical stories – one claimed to be homeless, the other a 'refugee' – and the Asian man was offered housing because his story fit the legal criteria better.[24] For the right, the BNP's emergence seemed to confirm their contention that immigration had been a disaster, and that local government was in the grip of politically-correct lunacy.

Worse still, all the negative attention generated by the BNP made it even less likely that the Isle of Dogs would receive the investment it sorely needed. Holtam, who had made representations to government on behalf of Islanders, said that some of the least creditable conversations he had 'were with a government minister and executives at the LDDC. All of them owned up to the problem [i.e., that underinvestment in social housing was at the root of BNP support], but they all said, "We can't be seen to be giving in to this sort of political pressure."' The LDDC executives in particular were terrified that an association with the BNP would jeopardise the whole Docklands project: 'I had a conversation with a senior executive on the board of the LDDC who said, "You've got to understand it from our point of view that if this ward votes BNP at the next election, this development is down the tube and all of the money that's been invested in here will simply go. The property will be left empty and nobody will want to work here."'

While LDDC executives worried about property deals, the people of Tower Hamlets were facing a more pressing problem as the borough experienced a resurgence of racist violence. On 8 September, an Asian teenager named Quddus Ali had been beaten into a coma in Whitechapel. On the afternoon of 19 September, a group of BNP activists, newly emboldened by their election victory, were drinking outside the Ship pub in Bethnal Green, when a black man, Stephen Browne, and his white girlfriend, Jenny Bone, tried to pass through the crowd on their way to the supermarket. The couple were spat at and showered with beer by BNP members, who shouted 'nigger lover' and 'monkey' at them. When the couple replied by telling the group to shut up and calling them cowards, the BNP's national organizer Richard Edmonds threw a glass. Others then 'glassed' Browne in the face and punched and kicked him as he lay on the ground. Browne was left scarred for life; Edmonds was later sentenced to three months in prison for his part in the assault.[25]

On the Isle of Dogs, police statistics showed a spike in 'recorded racial incidents', breaking the 100 barrier for the first time in 1993 and peaking at 180 in 1994.[26] Many Bengali families remained in their houses, scared to go out – and one man left altogether after a scaffolding pole was thrown through the glass of his front door.[27] 'After he [Beackon] was elected, we got really scared,' recalled Syeda Choudhury. 'I used to know white neighbours who would say hello to me in the street,' Choudhury said. 'They stopped. That's how bad it got.'

By 1993, Choudhury was married and had a one-year-old son, although the young family continued to live in her parents' council flat. Her husband was a student and used to work evening shifts at a restaurant, often returning home after midnight. So scared were the Choudhurys for his safety at night that they would escort him, en masse, from his car to the entrance of their tower block: 'He would phone us when he was leaving the restaurant, so me, my brother, my mum and my dad, all four of us, would have to go downstairs to where he'd park his car. We used to carry big sticks and a baseball bat. You could not have peace of mind all through the day and night. You were anxious, worried what's going to happen next.'

While the presence of the BNP sowed fear among the Island's Bengalis, it had also bred mutual suspicion among white residents. A white member of Holtam's congregation made a point of telling him that she hadn't voted for the party: 'I feel I've got to say that because I keep looking at people and wondering if they voted BNP.'

Who else might vote BNP, given the chance? Full council elections in Tower Hamlets were scheduled for May 1994, just eight months after the Millwall by-election. In the past, fascists had been driven off the streets of East London by diverse, grass-roots campaigns. In 1936 the Battle of Cable Street had blocked Oswald Mosley from leading his British Union of Fascists through Stepney – an area that then had a substantial Jewish population – thanks to a popular movement which embraced Jew and gentile, socialist and Communist. Four decades later, in the 1970s, white and black anti-racists fought street battles with the National Front. But this time, there was a difference: Derek Beackon had been elected. How on earth could the BNP's opponents influence what went on in the privacy of the polling booth?

At the end of September 1993, the *East London Advertiser* published an alarming statistic: 'More than 81 per cent support the BNP', claimed its front-page headline, trailing the result of a telephone poll in which readers had been asked, 'Do you think it is right or wrong that a BNP councillor has been elected to Tower Hamlets council?' The question was somewhat leading – in one sense, of course it was 'right'; Beackon had won a democratic election, and if you ignored the violence and intimidating behaviour of his party's supporters, then he had every right to take up his seat.

The *Advertiser*, a popular read among older white East Londoners, appeared to agree. On 5 October, after attending his first council meeting, Beackon told the paper it was 'full of figures and petty bickering. I'm an ordinary working-class bloke and most of the councillors are middle-class blokes, and for me it will take a little bit of understanding.' On 7 October, under a headline that read 'BNP's Beackon steps into family eviction storm', the *Advertiser* carried a report that claimed Beackon had helped 'fight off' bailiffs who wanted to evict 'asthmatic Geraldine Johnson' from her Isle of Dogs home. According to Nicholas Holtam, the paper's editor Richard Tidiman (who died in 2006), initially gave Beackon qualified support. 'Talking to the editor, he was worried about losing his readership. And of course the Bengalis don't read the *East London Advertiser*. His readership was declining and so the stories played to that perception of, "We white East Enders have got to stand up for what's right."'

While Beackon attempted to position himself as a people's champion, the borough's two main parties had fallen into bitter recriminations. In December, an inquiry ordered by the Lib Dem leader Paddy Ashdown recommended the expulsion of Jeremy Shaw – the former mayor who had told Bangladesh that his borough was 'full'. Its study of leaflets dating back to 1990 found that the party had 'pandered to racism', a conclusion that was disputed by local activists. Several prominent members tore up their party cards, while others branded Simon Hughes, the Bermondsey MP who had led the inquiry, as a 'back-stabber' and declared him 'persona non grata in the borough'.[28] A month later, a similar row erupted among Labour members, as the party debated whether to adopt a Lib Dem-style 'Sons and Daughters' housing policy in Millwall. After moves were made to expel its former candidate James Hunt for leaking the canvass return, a number of members resigned, Hunt included. He then announced he would stand as an independent.

In the absence of major parties, it was left to grassroots activists to build support for an anti-BNP campaign. Over the winter months, the Anti-Nazi League encouraged local firefighters, civil servants and health workers to leaflet against the BNP.[29]

Church volunteers, overseen by Holtam, worked with the Association of Island Communities to make sure that accurate information about housing and where council funds were being spent was distributed among Isle of Dogs residents.[30]

But they had competition: every Saturday morning, BNP canvassers would work the Island's estates, knocking on doors and telling white residents that Derek Beackon was available to fight their corner. Anti-fascist protesters had continued to picket council meetings that Beackon attended, and BNP canvassers would tell residents that he had been 'banned' from official buildings, but that he could make personal calls if they so desired.[31] Among voters who had already hit out once at the political establishment by electing Beackon, this merely reinforced the perception that they were being ignored. As Chuck, an Isle of Dogs resident, told me, it felt 'exactly the same as the Palestinian situation. You know, they all want democracy, they allow a democratic vote, then the wrong party gets in and nobody wants to work with them.'[32]

It wasn't until the spring of 1994 that the mainstream political parties began to campaign in earnest. The Lib Dems once more promoted a populist platform. The Tower Hamlets mayor, John Snooks, drew criticism from trade union leaders for ostentatiously displaying the Union Jack on his town hall desk. 'When it becomes a crime to love your country, I'll be the first to give myself up,' he said in reply. 'The only problem this borough faces is the cancer of the loony right and the loony left.'[33] In April, the Lib Dem-controlled council announced a 'carnival' parade through Tower Hamlets, intended to restore a sense of pride among inhabitants of the East End. Held on a hail-strewn, bitterly cold day, the parade was a nostalgic vision of pearly kings and queens, wooden-wheeled market stalls and horse-drawn traps – evoking a time, it might be noted, when London sat at the heart of a vast empire whose colonial subjects remained for the most part overseas. Trailing behind the rest of the thirty-five carnival floats, at the very back of the parade, came the Bangladesh Welfare Association.[34]

The same month, Labour unveiled a 'manifesto' for the Isle of Dogs. In the autumn of 1993, Frank Dobson, then shadow local government secretary, had been drafted in by the Labour leader John Smith to oversee the party's campaign. Dobson was convinced that the BNP could be beaten by a rejuvenated Labour campaign. 'The thing to remember about the BNP,' he told me, 'is that they're not eagles, they're vultures. If there's dead meat – useless councillors, people not pulling their weight, then that's where they succeed.' Dobson and another Labour MP, Nick Raynsford, held meetings throughout the autumn of 1993 with Island residents to find out what their concerns were; the manifesto promised more investment in housing if Labour were to win back control of the council. An ambitious young shadow minister named Tony Blair told an anti-racist rally in East London just a few weeks before the launch of the manifesto, 'We understand the problems are housing and jobs.'[35]

As polling day drew closer, a wide range of community groups emerged to boost turnout and to make sure people felt they were not alone in opposing the BNP. Holtam's church group distributed rainbow-coloured ribbons for people to wear. It was a small gesture, but as Holtam described it, the ribbons were 'symbolic, a positive statement that said we want to be part of a multiracial community. It gave the sense that they [the BNP] were not necessarily going to win it.' Syeda Choudhury's mother joined a group named Women Against Racism and set about convincing her Bengali friends on the Isle of Dogs to register to vote. Formed in

1993 as a response to the BNP, Women Against Racism brought female campaigners together from many ethnicities – white, Somali, Chinese and Asian. But as Julie Begum, one of the group's founders, explained, it drew on a strong tradition of anti-racist activism among East London's Bengalis: 'When our fathers and uncles and mothers arrived in the 60s, after the floods and the liberation war in Bangladesh, a lot of them were grateful for the refuge. Then in the 70s, there was an anger from young men who had grown up here, thinking, you know, we don't have to be killed, just because we're black. Since the 70s there's been much more of a resistance to racism and in the 90s I think that was revisited. A lot of people felt that they needed to come together again to respond to that racism.'

Finally, under pressure from campaigners, the *East London Advertiser* revised its position on the BNP. In a front-page story the week of the local elections, Richard Tidiman urged his readers to 'think about the consequences' of voting for the party. If they were unsure, then he suggested 'take a few hours off, go and see *Schindler's List*' before deciding.[36]

On 5 May, Derek Beackon's short reign was brought abruptly to an end. Labour swept the borough, wresting control of the council from the Lib Dems and winning all three seats in Millwall. But as Begum recalled it, this was less a party political victory than proof of what people could do by themselves: 'What I remember the most is our solidarity, the meetings – the sisterhood, if you like – of all these different women. We used to meet in our front rooms, making banners, producing posters and leaflets. There was lots of activity, we lived that time with each other constantly, in each others' houses, on the phone at demonstrations. It was exhausting, actually. And when we got the result, it was euphoric.'

Yet an uncomfortable truth remained. The BNP's vote had actually increased; spreading out across Tower Hamlets and into the neighbouring borough of Newham.[37] What sort of legacy would this dark period leave – for the Island; for Britain?

Summer 2011; I am sitting in on a pensioners' lunch club at a community hall on the Barkantine estate. Outside is bright sunshine, but as the diners finish their meal of savoury mince with dumplings, I am struck by the fact that the room's lights are on full. The housing association that now manages the estate has been selling off land to property speculators, who have erected a block of flats on what used to be the hall's back garden, blocking out any natural light. Now, they want to knock down the adjoining church. 'They said we could use a room on the second floor as a chapel,' Rita Bensley, lunch club organizer and a veteran Isle of Dogs community activist, tells me. 'I said, have you even checked to see if a coffin will fit in the lift? They hadn't.' Space, as ever, is at a premium on the Island.

After the plates are cleared, two of the group, Mary and Donna, settle down in a corner of the room with mugs of tea. I ask Mary how long she's lived here. 'I was born on the Island,' she says, 'and it got such a pounding in the war that my mum moved out to Stepney. But I moved back when I got married. In them days the Island was an "in" place to live – they were building all these new flats. I live on the twentieth floor and I've got a beautiful view. But now people can't get homes for their kids. It's not fair. I don't want to be called racist.'

'I think they should abolish that word, racist,' Donna interjects, fiercely. 'It's spot the white when you go down there –,' she gestures towards the other end of Barkantine. 'My grandson, his mum sent him to a lovely private school, but then they ran out of money and they sent him to the state primary here. Very mixed. His whole nature has changed. The way he talks, his attitude. He'd never have dreamed of that before.'

Mary nods. 'It might be a good school but it's not for our children.' She gives me a conspiratorial grin. 'It's like we've been invaded, only not with guns.'

After all this time, I ask, haven't people learned to mix?

'Well,' she replies. 'They never talk to us.'

2

Any Colour as Long as It's Black

After Millwall, debate gripped the BNP. Activists who had tramped the streets of London's East End and seen first hand what a few thousand low budget leaflets, false rumours and some doorstep cajoling could do, wanted the party to throw its efforts into more of the same. If only temporarily, Beackon's victory had shaken the idea that a vote for the BNP was a 'wasted' vote.

John Tyndall, the BNP's leader, wasn't so sure. He had tried the electoral route once before in the 1970s as chairman of the National Front and it had proved useless. This softly-softly approach wasn't really what being in a fascist party was about. For all the talk of fair treatment and housing allocations and equal rights to Tyndall, fascism was street politics, and a far-right party like the BNP could only bully its way into power. Looking for allies, Tyndall's attention lighted upon Nick Griffin, an activist who had recently been drawn into the BNP's orbit. 'The electors of Millwall', Griffin wrote in a party magazine, 'did not back a postmodernist rightist party, but what they perceived to be a strong, disciplined organisation with the ability to back up its slogan "Defend Rights for Whites" with well-directed boots and fists.'[1]

This was exactly what Tyndall wanted to hear – which should have made him wary. Griffin, then in his mid-thirties, had an arcane personal ideology formed from a soup of foreign and British intellectual traditions, along with a proven ability to switch allegiances at opportune moments. In nearly two decades of political activity, this chameleon had shown he could come in any colour, as long as it was black.

Born in 1959, in Barnet on the northern outskirts of London, Griffin was the son of right-wing Conservative Party activists (his father, Edgar, a small business owner, had met Nick's mother when they both turned up to heckle a Communist Party meeting in the early 1950s). Griffin received his early political education in the family home. It wasn't, perhaps, an entirely typical childhood: Griffin says that by the age of four-teen, he had read Hitler's *Mein Kampf*, although he has often claimed that only the chapter on propaganda made any lasting impression on him. Nevertheless, Griffin described his parents to me as mainstream Conservatives who were pushed right-wards by the Heath Government that came to power in 1970, and were 'increasingly dismayed by a Tory Government not doing anything to move the country back after Labour had ratcheted it leftwards.'

Above all, the issue that exercised the Griffins most, like many others on the Tory right, was immigration. For them, as for many others, the politics of the period were defined by the Tory MP Enoch Powell, in whose career were reflected the contortions of the British elite as it tried to reconcile itself to the loss of empire. Powell had set out as a vocal opponent of decol-onization, but when that came to nothing, he reinvented himself as a champion of the free market and the free movement of labour: during his stint as health minister in the late 1950s, he was one of the first to encourage nurses from former colonies to move to the UK. As late as 1964, he declared, 'I have set and always will set my face like flint against making any difference between one citizen of this country and another on grounds of his origin.' But when these new workers were not matched with expanded public services, Powell was one of the first to shape the resulting white resentment into a new political language.[2]

From 1965 onwards, Powell made a startling about-turn. After councillors in his Wolverhampton constituency expressed fears about the birth rate among non-whites in 1965, Powell demanded that Commonwealth immigrants be prevented from bringing their spouses and children into the country. When race riots in Detroit and other American cities erupted in the summer of 1967, he published a piece in the *Sunday Express* asking: 'Can We Afford to Let Our Race Problem Explode?' Then, in 1968, came a series of speeches that laid out the blueprint for anti-immigrant politics in the decades to come.

The first, delivered in Walsall on 9 February, conjured the image of a lone white child marooned in a classroom of immigrants. His misinterpretation of immigration statistics to back up his assertion foreshadowed the 'numbers game' now played by politicians across the spectrum. The second, in Birmingham on 20 April, was supported by an anecdote about an anonymous constituent, an elderly lady whose street had been overrun by blacks and who was now terrorised by 'grinning picaninnies' pushing excrement through her letter box. Another anonymous constituent, Powell claimed, had expressed the fear that 'in this country in fifteen or twenty years' time, the black man will have the whip hand over the white man.' The third, made in Eastbourne on 18 November, explicitly linked race and nation.

'The West Indian or Indian does not, by being born in England become an Englishman,' stated Powell. 'In law he becomes a United Kingdom citizen by birth; in fact he is a West Indian or an Asian still.' He invoked a 'mass of immigrants, living in their own communities, speaking their own languages and maintaining their native customs.'

This was a new kind of racism; a departure from the old, imperial kind that insisted on the biological superiority of whites. Powell recast whites as victims, under threat from alien cultures. His speeches, relayed to millions of people across the country who had never experienced immigration first-hand, appeared to confirm their worst fears about the presence of non-whites in British cities. They also contained many of the features of subsequent far-right propaganda: a vulnerable woman, dirt, the prospect of invasion. When Edward Heath dismissed Powell from the Shadow Cabinet, it sent many of his supporters on the Tory right hurtling towards a new political grouping, the National Front.

In October 1974, Edgar Griffin, now living in Suffolk, took his wife and two teenage children to a National Front meeting at a pub near the football ground in Norwich. In the pub's function room, in front of a genteel audience of about fifty people, a well-spoken young man gave a speech on immigration: why both main parties, Labour and Conservatives, would never stop the flow of immigrants and why the National Front was the only party committed to the repatriation of non-whites.

The NF, an alliance of ultra-conservatives, 'empire loyalists' and neo-Nazis that had formed in 1967, was the main beneficiary of the Powell affair. Aware that the larger part of their doctrine was shunned by the vast majority of the population, Britain's small network of fascists was constantly on the lookout for points where their ideas overlapped with mainstream opinion. Powell seemed to have provided one. As one of the NF's founders, John Bean, later recalled: 'Here was a leading, respectable, orthodox politician saying what we had said for more than a decade.'[3]

When Powell was condemned by his own party's leadership and dismissed from the Shadow Cabinet, recruits to the NF soared. As one former NF official claimed, 'Before Powell spoke, we were getting only cranks and perverts. After his speeches we started to attract, in a secret sort of way, the right-wing members of Tory organisations.'[4] The Heath Government responded by moving to the right on immigration policy, but this only provoked further demands for control. The NF experienced a further rise in support, particularly after the arrival in 1972 of Asian refugees from the former British colony of Uganda and at its peak claimed some 12,000 members – hardly a mass party, but unprecedented on the far right of British politics.

At the pub in Norwich, the fifteen-year-old Nick Griffin, then a pupil at the fee-paying Saint Felix school in Southwold, was impressed by what he heard. Ignoring his father's advice to join the Conservatives and work from within, he joined the National Front the following year, soon becoming secretary of the Ipswich branch.

During that period, the National Front was becoming increasingly dominated by a group of hardliners. The future BNP leader John Tyndall, initially barred from the NF because of his neo-Nazi activities, manoeuvred to take leadership of the party in 1972. In 1974, the year Griffin first attended an NF meeting, Tyndall established an 'Honour Guard' of young men to accompany the NF at marches and rallies. His intent, as he stated openly, was to mimic the propaganda techniques of the Third Reich:

> What is it that touches off a chord in the instincts of the people to whom we want to appeal? It can often be the most simple and primitive thing. Rather than a speech or printed article it may just be a flag; it may be a marching column; it may be the sound of a drum; it may be a banner or it may just be the impression of a crowd. None of these things contain in themselves one single argument, one single piece of logic . . . [instead] they are recognised as being among the things that appeal to the hidden forces of the human soul.[5]

In 1976, a more moderate faction, led by John Kingsley Read, split off to form the National Party, taking a chunk of the Tory-leaning membership with them. Griffin, however, stayed put.

Dominated by Tyndall and his sidekick Martin Webster, the National Front became more openly extreme. Tyndall would play the 'respectable' figurehead, addressing gatherings in a pompous oratorical style, while Webster would deliver rabble-rousing tirades aimed at the younger, more unruly supporters. As the 1970s drew on, the level of racist violence in areas where the NF was active soared.

At the end of 1977, Griffin — now studying history and law at Cambridge — attended a meeting at the National Front's headquarters in Leicester. Here, along with a working-class sixteen-year-old activist from Dagenham in East London named Joe Pearce, he was appointed to the governing body of a new group, the Young National Front. One of the Young National Front's first projects was to produce and distribute propaganda intended to undermine the growing anti-racist and anti-fascist movements. In 1976, the Rock Against Racism campaign had been established in response to rising anti-immigrant sentiment, encapsulated by comments made on stage by the rock musician Eric Clapton. The Anti-Nazi League was launched the following year, as alarm grew at the impact of the National Front. In January 1978, the Young National Front produced 250,000 leaflets aimed at schoolchildren titled 'How to spot a Red teacher'. The accompanying pamphlet, 'How to combat a Red teacher', suggested that teachers who promoted racial equality in the classroom, or denigrated nationalism in any way, were part of a Communist plot to take over the UK. Griffin's life at this point would revolve around his Cambridge studies during the week, and National Front activities at the weekends. Most often, he would travel to London, where he would spend his time at the party's headquarters in East London, providing 'security' or selling newspapers at the party's regular pitch just off Brick Lane in Whitechapel.

The NF, however, was already in decline. At its peak, in the 1977 elections for the Greater London Council, it received over 10 per cent of the vote in some boroughs,[6] but the party's morale was broken by a riot in Lewisham in August the same year, where its marchers were driven off the streets by a much larger Anti-Nazi League demonstration. Similar clashes over the following months drove away many more moderate supporters, some of whom were lured back to the Conservative Party in 1978 when its new leader, Margaret Thatcher, gave a television interview in which she described the fear of white Britons being 'swamped' by an alien culture. Not only did this stance draw some voters away from the NF; it indicated that the 'new' racism of Enoch Powell had now been repackaged and made part of the political mainstream. As Alfred Sherman, the former

Communist who had become one of Thatcher's closest advisors, wrote in the *Telegraph* that same year, 'It is from a recognition of racial difference that a desire develops in most groups to be among their own kind; and this leads to distrust and hostility when newcomers come in.'[7]

The NF performed abysmally in the 1979 general election, despite standing a record number of candidates. As a result Tyndall was ousted from the leadership by his erstwhile ally Martin Webster. Supporting Webster in this was Griffin, now part of a group of young activists who thought the NF needed to tailor its appeal more to alienated, urban working-class youth. They were known as the 'Strasserites'.

Attacking the free-market values of the Thatcher Government and calling for social security that guaranteed a basic standard of living – so long as you were white and British – the Strasserites took their name from two brothers who had been members of the German Nazi Party. Gregor and Otto Strasser were 'left-wing' Nazis who purported to side with workers against big business but rejected Communism as an anti-German plot. Griffin and other young NF members advocated Strasserite ideas through *Nationalism Today*, a magazine established as a counter to the official party journals in 1979.

One article, headlined 'We Are Not Marxists – We Are Not Capitalists', promised 'radical ideological development' of the NF's programme:

> We reject the Marxist belief that human consciousness and social structures have their ultimate origins in changing economic relations and that a future change in economic relations will lead to a new human type and to a new society free

from antagonism of any kind. We reject the Capitalist prescription that political man must make way for economic man and that our decisions, personal as well as political, should be made on economic grounds; that we should live in order to work, rather than work in order to live.[8]

Did this make the NF Strasserites 'left-wing'? The short answer is no, since racial purity and private property took precedence over any egalitarian commitment. They combined the Strassers' ideas with the creed of Distributism, an economic theory that grew from a tradition of English radical right-wing thought in the early twentieth century. It held that the political elite acted only in the interests of an international 'plutocracy' and that the solution lay in an equal distribution of private property among the national community. These ideas were first explored by the journalist Hilaire Belloc in *The Party System* (1911), which argued that both Liberal and Tory parliamentary front benches had more in common with one another – serving the interests of big business – than with their own membership. *The Servile State* (1912) argued that state welfare provision would only end up enslaving the working class.

After the First World War, Belloc's ideas were taken up and shaped into the creed of Distributism by his friend G.K. Chesterton. It looked back to a heavily idealized medieval Christian Europe of peasants, where craftsmen and merchants were organized into guilds that set prices and regulated competition. According to Chesterton, the advent of capitalism, which was unstable and put wealth in the hands of a few, only undermined this. He argued that every English family should own its own means of production, as a guarantee of economic independence and liberty.[9]

For the National Front Strasserites, Distributism conveniently provided a bridge between mainstream political thought and their own racism. Not only did it give a 'patriotic' gloss to their ideas, but Chesterton's distrust of Bolshevism and 'cosmopolitan finance' had at times shaded into anti-Semitic conspiracy theory. Such anti-Semitism had always been a feature of far-right doctrine in the UK, and the Strasserites were no exception. Capitalism and 'national independence' could not coexist, they argued; the sovereignty of the nation state must be protected from the 'Money Power'. During one of our interviews, Griffin readily admitted to the anti-Semitic nature of the Strasserite programme: 'Our position . . . was the leftist SA[10] position where they happily allied themselves with the Communists and said well as regards the banks we'll shoot the Jewish ones and you shoot the rest.' He laughed. 'Fairly pragmatic.'

Past issues of *Nationalism Today* are full of anti-Semitic caricatures: in one, a cigar-smoking, hook-nosed businessman is blamed for acid rain in an illustration accompanying an article titled 'Capitalism Poisons Europe'.[11] Numerous articles about 'black crime' (a favourite 1970s NF propaganda theme) appear along with adverts for *The Turner Diaries*, a novel by the American white supremacist William Luther Pierce in which he imagines a violent revolution and ensuing race war in the United States. The novel has inspired neo-Nazis around the world – most notably Timothy McVeigh, who bombed a government building in Oklahoma City in April 1995.

The day-to-day reality of the National Front in the 1980s was more prosaic. It had been smashed as a serious political force, while Webster continued to recruit the most thuggish elements to its cause. Its propaganda was based on crude racism and little else. Under Webster's direction, the Young National Front launched a youth magazine, *Bulldog*, aimed at the skinhead subculture and edited by Pearce, who spent two spells in prison for incitement to racial hatred as a result. It also established a music venture, White Noise, which promoted 'white power' punk rock and was centred on the racist skinhead band Skrewdriver. Griffin organized festivals for Skrewdriver and other bands on his parents' land in Suffolk. Webster's leadership lasted until 1983, before he too was forced out of the National Front – by the Strasserites. This heralded yet another ideological twist.

Run by a couple of well-spoken graduates named Nick and Michael, on the face of it Heritage Tours seemed much like any other company offering to take tourists on trips around London's landmarks during the mid-1980s. But away from the day job, the 'guides' were committed racial nationalists, working to formulate a political creed that combined 'revolutionary' rhetoric, fascist mysticism and ideas about building a social movement derived in part from Marxist philosophy.

Heritage Tours was run from the central London flat of Michael Walker – one of several money-making schemes Griffin took part in to fund his political activities. Walker, a former regional organizer of the NF and a talented linguist, was convinced that the British far right lacked theory. He developed an interest in ideas circulating among a group of intellectuals within the French far-right Front National, associated with the *Groupement de recherches et d'études pour la civilisation européenne* (the Research and Study Group for European Civilization) or GRECE. Led by the philosopher Alain de Benoist, GRECE attacked what it saw as the soulless nature of consumer capitalism. Liberal, multiracial America was seen as the worst embodiment of this phenomenon, against which de Benoist advocated a revival of European national cultures. Rather than arguing for the superiority of one race over another, he maintained the issue was one of difference: keeping races and cultures separate would lead to a national spiritual rebirth and end the alienation of contemporary life.[12]

De Benoist also took ideas about strategy from the Italian Communist Antonio Gramsci. Drawing on Gramsci's 'war of position' theory, he argued that the far right needed to achieve cultural hegemony before it could gain political power, pushing key ideas and values among groups of influential people. As the GRECE journal *Eléments* explained, 'We want to attract those few thousand people who make a country tick. A few thousand is not many in absolute terms, but a few thousand of such importance, sharing the same thoughts and methods, represent the potential for revolution.'[13]

Meanwhile, Heritage Tours became the subject of a press exposé thanks to the involvement of Roberto Fiore, a friend of Griffin's.[14] Only a few months older than Griffin, he had fled to London from Italy with the help of the League of St George, a clandestine far-right network that provided 'safe houses' for neo-Nazis on the run. Fiore, despite maintaining his innocence, was wanted by Italian police because of his association with a terrorist group, the Nuclei Armati Rivoluzionari (Armed Revolutionary Nuclei), which had bombed a Bologna train station in 1980, killing eighty-five people.

Fiore was part of a new generation of Italian fascists who rejected parliamentary politics, looking instead to the ideas of the Sicilian mystic philosopher Julius Evola (1898–1974). Like de Benoist, Evola had criticized the decadence of capitalist society, but for him, spiritual rebirth would be achieved by an elite warrior caste. Fiore had used Evola's ideas to formulate a creed he called Terza Posizione, which like the Strasserites claimed to take up a 'third' position that was neither Capitalist nor Communist, and sought to achieve its goals by building grass-roots social movements.

When Fiore arrived in Britain, he was looking for activists among whom he could spread Third Positionist ideas and struck up a friendship with Griffin, who was impressed by the Italian's knowledge and organizational experience. Together with two other young National Front members, Derek Holland and Patrick Harrington, the group became known as the 'Political Soldiers', after a manifesto written by Holland and published in 1984. Claiming that the white race was under threat and the 'death of Europe' was at hand, the manifesto called for activists 'to be moulded into National Revolutionary Warriors', and to become a new type of man 'who will live the Nationalist way of life every day'. The manifesto concluded with the exhortation 'Long Live Death!', a slogan derived from Evola.[15]

Such rhetoric proved unpalatable to many NF members and the party split in 1986, with the Political Soldiers naming their faction the Official National Front. They further elaborated their theory of race, arguing that 'the racialist position now adopted by the National Front is based on the Nationalist principle that self-rule and the preservation of racial and cultural identity is the inalienable right of all the people of the world.'[16] Following this logic, they began to adopt the language of black separatist and Third World liberation movements, professing support for the Iranian Revolution and Palestinian freedom. The Political Soldiers heaped praise on the Libyan leader Muammar Gaddafi's Jamahiriya theory of direct democracy, claiming 'the very ideology which we hold dear is articulated in a superbly concise and direct manner in the pages of [Gaddafi's] *Green Book*.'[17] They also applauded the 'true democracy' of the Libyan People's Committee and Gaddafi's 'belief in the inalienable right to self-determination of all the races of mankind'. The *Green Book*, then, was 'essential reading for all who share our vision'. Griffin and Holland travelled to the Libyan capital Tripoli in search of financial support from Gaddafi, who at the time was funding a range of groups who opposed Western governments. They returned empty-handed, save for a couple of crates of the revered volume.

Beyond their own dwindling circle, the Political Soldiers had little impact. Unsuccessful attempts were made to set up a housing co-op in Northern Ireland in 1986 and, later, to infiltrate the anarchist squatters' movement in Hackney, East London.[18] The Official National Front increasingly came to resemble a cult: selected groups of recruits were reportedly taken for ideological cadre 'training' on Griffin's parents' land, while slogans such as 'Fight Racism' rapidly alienated members who had not kept up with the pace of change. When the March 1988 edition of the party newspaper featured pictures of Gaddafi, Iran's Ayatollah Khomeini and the US black separatist Louis Farrakhan on the front cover, it provoked a wave of resignations from the party.

The Official National Front disbanded in 1989 and Griffin's clique renamed itself the International Third Position. They began buying dilapidated properties in rural France and renovating them: Griffin describes this as purely a business venture but others have claimed it was an attempt to set up a commune.[19] At the same time he was becoming politically estranged from Holland and Fiore, both of whom were Catholics, and were introducing an increasing amount of religious rhetoric into the ITP's doctrine.

In March 1990, Griffin says he was stacking a bonfire at one of the properties in France when he accidentally threw some shotgun cartridges onto the fire. One apparently exploded, seriously injuring Griffin and blinding him in one eye. He was forced to return to convalesce at home with his parents, who were almost bankrupted after they had bailed him out of a property deal gone wrong. For the time being, Griffin disappeared from active politics. He had achieved nothing, but the ideas he had toyed with would later resurface as he manoeuvred to take over the BNP.

3

The Führer of Notting Hill

In the spring of 1964, an American journalist named George Thayer visited a run-down property in Notting Hill, West London. Researching a book on Britain's fringe parties, he had been granted an audience with John Tyndall, leader of the recently formed Greater Britain Movement. At 76 Princedale Road Thayer found a forbidding building, with steel shutters and wire mesh covering the ground floor windows. Swastikas had been painted on the brickwork, high out of reach of the street, which bore splashes of paint that had been thrown during a recent scuffle with opponents.

Once inside, Thayer was ushered in to a small back room, adorned with a portrait of Adolf Hitler, and found Tyndall: 'He was a composite of all the characteristics I had vaguely associated with Nazis in Hitler's Germany,' wrote Thayer. 'He had cold, evasive eyes, was blond and balding, and had not the slightest spark of humour. He was suspicious, nervous, and excitable, and moved with all the stiffness of a Prussian in Court.'

'Jewry,' Tyndall announced to Thayer, 'is a world pest wherever it is found in the world. The Jews are more clever and more financially powerful than other people and have to be eradicated before they destroy the Aryan peoples.'

Tyndall went on to explain that his party was seeking to imbue the ideas of Hitler with specifically British characteristics. Details, however, were sketchy, and at the time of the meeting the only concrete proposal was that the swastika armbands worn by members inside the Princedale Road HQ – to wear them outside would have fallen foul of public order laws – would be blue, rather than the traditional red. 'It will be interesting,' mused Thayer, 'to see how he combines the qualities of National Socialism with those of John Bull.'[1]

There were two guiding stars in John Tyndall's political universe: Adolf Hitler and the British Empire. Born in 1934, and subsequently a pupil at Beckenham and Penge grammar school in south-east London, he was an undistinguished scholar who spent most of his spare time playing football and cricket, or indulging his passion for fitness. After completing his national service, he flirted briefly with left-wing politics, even visiting a world youth festival in the Soviet Union, before moving swiftly to the right. Tyndall's conversion, he would later claim, was motivated by disgust at the idea that the British, a nation bound by 'bonds of race', as he saw it, might recognize colonial subjects as equals. In this belief, he found a home in a group called the League of Empire Loyalists.[2]

As the name suggests, the League's origins lay in a backlash against the decline of Imperial Britain. Formed in 1954, it was not the first far-right group to emerge after the Second World War – that was the Union Movement, formed in 1948 by the former British Union of Fascists leader Oswald Mosley and what remained of his supporters – but it was the first to have an impact on mainstream political life.

A pressure group rather than a political party, the League

campaigned against the 'Butskellite'[3] consensus of the 1950s and early 1960s that saw both Labour and Conservative parties adapt, if reluctantly, to reduced influence abroad and the social democratic principles of the welfare state at home. The group's modus operandi was to disrupt political speeches and public events with heckling and elaborate stunts. Members blew bugles during meetings, hid under speakers' platforms overnight so they could burst out mid-speech, or bluffed their way in to receptions for visiting dignitaries.

But there was a more sinister edge to the League. The group, which brought together retired military officials and former colonial administrators with the right-wing Tory fringe, also provided a new home for fascists. Its founder was A.K. Chesterton, a cousin of the writer G.K. Chesterton, who had been a propagandist for Mosley's British Union of Fascists until 1938. A.K. Chesterton fought for Britain against the Nazis during the war, but he was deeply anti-Semitic and a fervent believer in white racial superiority.

By Tyndall's account, it was during his time in the League of Empire Loyalists that he was introduced to 'the conspiracy theory', via the pages of Chesterton's magazine *Candour*. He also encountered the League's West Midlands organizer, Colin Jordan, a young history teacher who was using the League as cover for other activities. Jordan was a disciple of Arnold Leese, the founder of the pro-Hitler Imperial Fascist League, which before the war had scorned the 'kosher fascists' of Mosley's BUF. Leese had a visceral hatred of Jews, stemming, he claimed, from the methods of ritual slaughter he witnessed while stationed in the Middle East as a colonial veterinary surgeon. He was interned during the war, returning to prison in 1947 for helping former Waffen-SS members flee Europe. After his release, Leese promoted his views in his magazine *Gothic Ripples*, through which he caught the attention of Jordan.

Under the tutelage of Leese, who died in 1956, Jordan formed a neo-Nazi secret circle called The Ring, which painted bridges and viaducts calling for the release from prison of Hitler's former deputy Rudolph Hess.[4] He also gathered followers for his paramilitary White Defence League, members of which physically attacked black immigrants in Birmingham and London. Given a base at Princedale Road by Leese's widow, Jordan joined other far-right groups in encouraging anti-black feeling before and after the 1958 Notting Hill race riots.

Tyndall fell into Jordan's orbit and absorbed the theory, inherited from Leese, that Jews were encouraging non-white immigration in order to dilute Britain's racial stock. By 1957, limited by the Blimpish posturing of the League, Tyndall left and formed the National Labour Party. In 1960, this merged with Jordan's White Defence League to form the first British National Party, headquartered at Princedale Road.

This British National Party of the early 1960s did not fight elections with any seriousness; rather, it aimed to attract publicity and build up support in the traditional fascist manner, by holding marches, rallies and street-corner gatherings, particularly in Jewish areas of East London. (The size of these should not be overstated: many attracted only a handful of supporters, and were treated with indifference, or contempt, by many passers-by.) What distinguished the British National Party from its predecessors, however, was that it made opposition to non-white immigration its central pitch, calling for an immediate halt and proposing the repatriation of non-whites already in the country. These demands would be at the heart of every subsequent far-right movement.

In what would become a familiar pattern, Tyndall had made alliances by playing down his more extreme tendencies,[5] but it rapidly became apparent that both Tyndall and Jordan were primarily interested in recreating the Third Reich, if only in their own imaginations. Tyndall would reputedly travel across London to party meetings wearing jackboots under his trousers.[6] Jordan, as head of the British National Party's External Department, was preoccupied with 'white world solidarity' and busied himself building up contacts with neo-Nazis in Europe, the US and Australia.[7]

In May 1960, the British National Party held a summer camp on the Norfolk estate of its president, Andrew Fountaine. Here, among ceremonies steeped in Nordic mystic fantasy (the opening event was the lighting of an 'Aryan sunwheel'),[8] Jordan and Tyndall unveiled a uniformed group of militants, modelled on Hitler's SA, that they had named Spearhead. Dressed in grey shirts, Sam Browne belts and jackboots, Spearhead members met regularly at Princedale Road for 'training'. Throughout the summers of 1960 and 1961 they would camp in various rural locations around England to practice marching, unarmed combat and 'securing vital bridgeheads'.[9] Some of their colleagues were alarmed at this development and in January 1962 both Tyndall and Jordan were expelled from the party.

That year, on 20 April – Adolf Hitler's birthday – the pair launched the National Socialist Movement. As Tyndall recalled, the party took its name 'directly from the Hitler party in Germany, together with a programme that in all the essential respects was the same.'[10] The National Socialist Movement never numbered more than a hundred or so members, but the very fact of its existence, in a country that only twenty years previously had been at war with Nazi Germany, generated a certain level of public notoriety.

In July, the National Socialist Movement held a rally in Trafalgar Square, at which Tyndall stated 'the Jew is like a poisonous maggot'. Jewish war veterans and other anti-fascists stormed the platform and Tyndall was sentenced to a month in prison for breach of the peace. The same summer, Jordan held a gathering of international neo-Nazis at a 'secret' location at Temple Guiting in Gloucestershire. In attendance was the leader of the American Nazi Party, George Lincoln Rockwell, along with representatives of neo-Nazi parties from across Europe. The ensuing 'Cotswold Declaration' established a World Union of National Socialists.

The scandalized press coverage of these events led to a police raid on the NSM headquarters at Princedale Road and Jordan's home in Coventry, where weapons were seized, along with cans of weed-killer, one of which had had its label altered to read 'Jew killer'. Jordan, Tyndall and two other NSM members were sentenced to prison under the 1936 Public Order Act – which had banned the wearing of political uniforms and the training of paramilitaries – for their Spearhead activities. The lasting significance of the Spearhead trial was that from then on, 'legitimate' parties would have to publicly disassociate themselves from violent activity, even if they continued to hold covert links.[11]

Two years later, the NSM split, due to a falling-out between Jordan and Tyndall over the affections of Françoise Dior, a wealthy heiress and niece of the French fashion designer Christian Dior. While Tyndall was still in prison, she married Jordan, in a ritualistic ceremony. For the occasion, Dior 'wore a black and gold swastika necklace, encrusted with diamonds. They supped mead, toasted the British Nazi movement to the strains of the *Horst Wessel Lied* [the German Nazi Party's anthem], and over a swastika draped table, swore that they were of untainted Aryan blood, cut their fingers and let the mingled drop of blood fall on to an open page of a virgin copy of Hitler's *Mein Kampf*.' [12] Tyndall left, to form his own Greater Britain Movement in the spring of 1964.

That year, disturbed by what he had found on his visit to Princedale Road, the journalist Thayer suggested that Tyndall and Jordan's activities were 'more the concern of psychiatrists than the concern of political observers'. Indeed, they might have remained an unpleasant but meaningless historical foot-note had the wider politics of immigration not taken a sudden turn for the worse.

Smethwick, an industrial town just west of Birmingham where many Commonwealth immigrants – chiefly Indian Sikhs – settled during the 1950s, holds an infamous place in the history of race relations. In 1964, the Conservative Party candidate Peter Griffiths caused one of the upsets of that year's general election when he unseated the former Labour minister Patrick Gordon Walker with a virulently anti-immigrant campaign. In particular, Griffiths had benefited from a racist slogan circulated in the town before the election: 'If you want a nigger neighbour, vote Labour'. It never appeared on official Conservative Party election litera-ture, but Griffiths refused to condemn the slogan, describing it as 'a manifestation of popular feeling'. [13]

In fact, this was early evidence of the role that far-right parties can play in altering the course of mainstream politics. The 'nigger neighbour' slogan had been coined by an activist in Oswald Mosley's Union Movement and was circulated by vari-ous fascist groups, including the post-Tyndall British National

Party. Griffiths was labelled a 'political leper' for his campaign by the incoming prime minister, Harold Wilson, but the shock of Smethwick helped push the Labour Government to further tighten immigration controls and introduce the first race relations laws by way of compensation.

In 1960s Britain it was clear to all but the handful of obsessives who surrounded Tyndall that the pre-war fascist traditions had been as good as extinguished. But anti-immigrant racism was very much alive, and this new-found ability to affect the outcome of elections – in however limited a way – provided an incentive to pool resources. In 1966 A. K. Chesterton, now in his seventies, began discussions to merge his much-diminished League of Empire Loyalists with a number of other groups. In 1967, the League joined with the British National Party and a pressure group called the Racial Preservation Society to form the National Front, numbering about 1,500 active members in total.[14]

Chesterton initially told Tyndall he would not be allowed to join the party, because of his neo-Nazism, but Tyndall was determined to charm his way in. He published a manifesto, *Six Principles of British Nationalism* (1966), which modified his authoritarian views just enough to declare that any government must 'function under the terms of British democracy'. Tyndall then disbanded his Greater Britain Movement and instructed members to join the National Front. He joined them several months later.

Almost immediately, Tyndall set about exploiting divisions among the leadership of the fledgling National Front. First, he sided with A. K. Chesterton in a personality clash with Andrew Fountaine, the former British National Party president. In 1968, with Tyndall's support, Chesterton expelled

Fountaine from the party. Two years later, Tyndall's faction forced A. K. Chesterton out of the party, and in 1972 he installed himself as chairman.

Tyndall's claim to have moderated his views was merely expedient. Under his leadership, the National Front became more openly fascist in character and after its implosion in 1979, Tyndall was forced out. He formed the New National Front, primarily to retain a circle of followers while he decided what to do next. An opportunity came in the form of Colin Jordan's National Socialist Movement, which had been renamed the British Movement in 1968. Jordan's own political career, such as it was, had ended in ignominy in 1975, when he was arrested for shoplifting women's underwear from a West Midlands branch of Tesco, but his British Movement had lived on, making a name for itself as a violent skinhead street gang. In 1981, Tyndall was approached by Ray Hill, a leader of the British Movement. Hill proposed a merger, describing this new project, in the political language of the 1980s, as an 'SDP of the far right'.[15]

Unaware that Hill was in fact working as a mole for the anti-fascist organization Searchlight, and was intending to further fragment the far right, Tyndall was attracted by the offer. By Hill's account, Tyndall declared that 'nationalism' was 'never going to make it through the ballot box' and that this new party's aim should be 'to build an organization of 5,000 "solid types" which could be put out on to the streets at any time'.[16]

This, then, was the genesis of the party which Nick Griffin would later lead: a lineage of the most extreme sections of the British far right, and structured according to what is sometimes termed the 'Führer principle', with absolute control invested in the role of leader. In April 1982, the modern British National

Party was launched at a press conference near London's Victoria station. The first task was to gain publicity: later that year, activists disrupted a recording of the BBC's *Question Time* and the BNP stood enough candidates at the 1983 general election to qualify for a five-minute TV and radio broadcast.

But there was no gap in the market for right-wing nationalism. While anti-fascists had eroded the organizational capacity of the National Front in the late 1970s, Margaret Thatcher had stolen their ideological clothing. As prime minister, she had successfully held together a coalition of support with her blend of jingoism and watered-down Powellism. Tyndall, as he had stated in his Six Principles, may have aimed to save Britain from 'a crisis of national existence', but in 1983 Thatcher had grasped the narrative of imperial decline and turned it to her advantage after the Falklands war. Why, some of her opponents might have asked, would Britain need another authoritarian demagogue dedicated to smashing the left – there was one in Downing Street already, wasn't there?

After 1983, Tyndall focused the BNP's efforts on recruiting supporters and worked to infiltrate the few areas of the Conservative Party that looked as if they might be susceptible. In the mid-80s, one was the Monday Club, an anti-immigration pressure group, which had drifted further rightwards since its formation in the 1960s. The other was the Federation of Conservative Students, which had been taken over by a group of young libertarians including the future speaker of the House of Commons, John Bercow. The FCS was gaining notoriety for provocative slogans such as 'Hang Mandela', referring to the leader of the South African liberation struggle and hurled at opponents of the Apartheid regime.[17]

There appeared to be an opportunity to forge links with Tory students in May 1985 when Paul Staines, an FCS activist at Humberside College, wrote a letter to the BNP organizer in Hull proposing 'direct action' to disrupt left-wing meetings. It was a false lead. Staines – now a prominent commentator on Westminster affairs, better known as the political blogger Guido Fawkes – says he was on a 'fishing expedition', hoping to find information he could use against the BNP.[18]

In July, however, an Essex University graduate named Stuart Millson, who was a regional chairman of the FCS and chairman of the Monday Club's student group, announced he was defecting to the British National Party. Another FCS member, Austin Redmond, told the *Guardian*: 'Quite a few of my members do support the BNP. I support the BNP on most issues, including law and order and race relations and immigration.' Minutes of a Monday Club immigration and repatriation committee, meanwhile, revealed a commitment to ending 'New Commonwealth and Pakistan immigration, a properly financed system of voluntary repatriation, the repeal of the Race Relations Act and the abolition of the Commission for Racial Equality. Particular emphasis on repatriation.'[19]

Such sympathies were limited, however – not least because the BNP did not hide its extremism. In 1986, Tyndall and the editor of the BNP newspaper were each sentenced to a year in prison for conspiracy to incite racial hatred after publishing attacks on blacks, Jews and Asians.[20] Propaganda from this period also aimed to exploit local racial tensions. After a string of arson attacks on Asian families in Ilford, East London – including one that killed a mother and her three sons on 13 July 1985 – the BNP began fly-posting notices calling for the repatriation of blacks and Asians. The party's local organizer, Tony Lecomber, admitted to the *Guardian* that some BNP supporters had been involved in racial violence.[21] A year later, Lecomber himself was given a three-year prison sentence after a bomb he made – packed with nails and hidden in a biscuit tin – exploded by accident in his car as he was driving through South London near the headquarters of the Workers Revolutionary Party.

By 1987, the BNP was so beleaguered that it did not stand any candidates at the general election. But almost by default, as Griffin's Political Soldiers were leading what remained of the National Front into the exotic territory of 'revolutionary' Third Positionism, the next few years saw it emerge as the most prominent group on the British far right.

In June 1989, the BNP held a rally in Dewsbury, West Yorkshire, in support of white parents who had withdrawn their children from a school where most pupils happened to be Asian. As Tyndall had no doubt hoped, it ended in violence, with Asian youths attacking the Dewsbury pub where children of the boycott organizers had been temporarily schooled. The ensuing media coverage indicated that the BNP had now overtaken the National Front in the public eye. In theory, this should have been a situation ripe for exploitation. Attention was already trained on British Asian Muslims and had been since copies of Salman Rushdie's 1988 novel *The Satanic Verses* were publicly burned earlier that year in nearby Bradford, leading to fierce controversy over the book's publication. A far-right demagogue of the twenty-first century might have exploited the issue with a rally defending Rushdie's right to 'free speech' and a media-friendly leader explaining to the TV news that they were not racist, only opposing Muslim 'extremism'. Instead, the episode merely revealed Tyndall's limitations as a leader.

As Eddy Butler, the East London activist who had joined the

BNP in 1986 and was at the Dewsbury rally, remembered: 'We had a crowd of about a thousand people all from Leeds and Dewsbury and he lost them completely. He knew how to talk to a small room of nationalists, but he didn't know how to talk to a thousand Yorkshire young geezers. He hadn't got a clue about normal people or normal politics. He'd go on about the Britain of Sir Francis Drake; you'd think "what's he on about?"'

By the end of the 80s, the policies of Thatcher had unleashed a tidal wave of social and economic destruction that engulfed Britain's industrial towns. Many 'working-class Tories' who shared the values touted by Thatcher would look at the wreckage around them and swear never to vote Conservative again. Perhaps a nimble operator, knowing which parts of his doctrine should or should not be aired in public, could tailor propaganda in a way that might attract some of these disillusioned voters.

John Tyndall, lover of Nazi pageantry, was not that kind of politician. His speeches were pompous but studied – based on careful observation of Adolf Hitler's oratorical style. Tyndall copied the hand gestures, the rising delivery that ended in a crescendo of angry epithets, adding evocations of British troops 'who spilled their blood on the battlefields of Burma and Africa'. But it was flat and tedious, like a provincial PE teacher trying to show his bored pupils how the rugby or football greats might have done it.

Butler's final assessment of his former leader was candid: 'He was a determined person and he had staying power, but that's about it really. He could speak well and look well, and a lot of people in politics think if you can speak well and look the part – it's image and presentation, isn't it? But there wasn't a lot behind it. He just wasn't that clever.'

4

Forget about the Ideas and Think about Selling Them

In the autumn of 1991, after a year's convalescence following his mishap with the shotgun cartridges, Nick Griffin made his return to far-right politics. On 14 November, sporting a patch to cover his injured eye,[1] he appeared at the Old Town Hall in Chelsea, in charge of the security team for a talk by an American designer of execution chambers named Fred Leuchter.[2] Without a party, and without allies, after his falling out with the NF Political Soldiers, Griffin needed to re-establish his credibility on the far right. Leuchter was promoting a book 'proving' that killings by gas did not take place at Auschwitz and Griffin had latched on to a cottage industry, small but thriving in the early 1990s: Holocaust denial.

With the end of the Second World War, and the ensuing revelations of the full horror of the Nazi concentration camps, the biggest obstacle to any far-right movement seeking to broaden its appeal was the legacy of the Holocaust. Among neo-Nazis, public revulsion at the greatest crime of the twentieth century has been attributed to Jewish manipulation of the media. Consequently, much effort has been devoted to keeping anti-Semitic conspiracy theory alive – using falsifications such as *The Protocols of the Elders of Zion*, which purported to be a

Jewish plan for world domination – and to questioning the extent or even the existence of the Holocaust itself with such documents as the widely distributed pamphlet *Did Six Million Really Die?* (1979). Unlike elsewhere in Western Europe, Britain never passed laws banning Holocaust denial, so by 1991 it had long been a production hub for anti-Semitic literature, much of it emanating from the Historical Review Press, a publisher with close links to the BNP.[3]

In the early 90s, the subject was being pursued with a renewed vigour. The collapse of the USSR had opened up a new potential market in former Eastern Bloc countries, where the legacy of the Holocaust had never been as openly discussed. In Britain, for the first time since the war, fascists were being given a fleeting opportunity to push their ideas into the mainstream, via the right-wing historian David Irving. Once a respected historian, he had published several books on the Second World War, but had moved into increasingly questionable territory. By 1991 he was openly disputing the scale of the Nazi genocide, yet did not lose his mainstream respectability straight away; in 1992, he was hired by the *Sunday Times* to supply the newspaper with previously unseen parts of Joseph Goebbels's diaries – and used his position to support others with similar opinions. It was with Irving's help that the American Auschwitz 'expert' Leuchter, banned from entering the UK by the home secretary, had been smuggled into the country by car.[4]

Griffin spied an opportunity, and spent the years that followed attempting to establish himself as an authority on Holocaust denial. He gave speeches at BNP meetings where he would say that Irving was 'soft' on numbers and that even fewer Jews had been killed than the historian claimed.[5] It was in this guise that Eddy Butler recalled his first encounter with Griffin, at a BNP meeting in London in 1993, shortly before the Isle of Dogs by-election victory: 'Griffin comes to this meeting and says "Irving's nobody, he knows nothing, I'm the expert on this subject and Irving's a bloody sellout traitor because he admits some of it happened; I'm saying none of it happened." So he's setting himself up as the real true unadulterated pure Holocaust revisionist and Irving as a charlatan.'

Griffin confirmed to me that he tried to outflank Irving, although he claims never to have disputed that 'the Nazis and their allies murdered huge numbers of Jews just because they were Jews'. Instead, he rationalized his stance by adding: 'I felt that this thing [the Holocaust] was being used to stifle argument as a huge moral club which anyone who asks questions of immigration or opposition to globalism is beaten up with . . . I thought, this club has to be broken.'

Griffin was not a newcomer to anti-Semitic conspiracy theory, but a renewed emphasis on Holocaust denial was an effective strategy by which Griffin could once again earn the respect of his peers. As Butler put it: 'In nationalism, you're judged on the degree of your intellect, by the extent of your anti-Semitism and how much you understand the nature of the world-wide Jewish conspiracy.'

At their meeting in 1993, Griffin was also scornful of the BNP's small steps towards electoral politics, telling Butler that it was a waste of time. Yet within only a few years Griffin would have made a complete U-turn, arguing that the BNP needed to 'modernize' its image in order to fight elections. How did this happen?

By the end of 1993, John Tyndall was struggling to contain the results of a plan that had backfired. Since the Spearhead trial of

1962, far-right parties had been forced to publicly distance themselves from paramilitary activity, but this did not mean that Tyndall had given up on the idea – the fact that he titled his own magazine *Spearhead*, published until his death in 2005, should be evidence enough. Instead, it would have to be achieved at arm's length.

As the BNP rose to prominence at the turn of the 1990s, its activities brought unwelcome attention from anti-fascists, who would violently break up party meetings with a level of success that threatened the BNP's capacity to function. In 1991, a group of younger BNP members and skinheads from East London formed a gang called the East End Barmy Army, in order to fight the left – and carry out random attacks on blacks and Asians. Early in 1992, it was decided that the Barmy Army needed to be brought into the fold. On behalf of Tyndall, Eddy Butler met with the gang and proposed founding an 'elite' group of BNP stewards. But their leader, a former British Movement member named Charlie Sargent, demanded a more independent organization. This was named Combat 18.[6]

Inspired by the American white supremacist Harold Covington and openly neo-Nazi, the group rapidly became a problem for the BNP. Convinced of the need for a violent uprising against the state; a 'race war' of the kind outlined in the white supremacist novel *The Turner Diaries*, Combat 18 turned on those BNP activists who favoured electoral politics (Butler himself was later slashed in the face by Combat 18 members). After the Millwall victory in late 1993, Tyndall declared Combat 18 a proscribed organization, but it was too late: the following year, as morale sagged after failure at the local elections in May, when Derek Beackon lost his seat on the Isle of Dogs, younger activists continued to drift away from the BNP towards Combat 18.[7]

With Butler's election-friendly wing of the party threatening a leadership challenge, Tyndall was desperate to boost his support among hardliners. It was at this point that he began to receive letters from Griffin, expressing an interest in working more closely with the BNP. Griffin had already been writing articles for BNP-linked magazines, arguing for unity among the fragmented far right, and advocating what he now calls a 'hardline and principled' stance. This meant opposing the faction, centred around Butler, that argued that the BNP had to soften its stance on immigration and drop its flagship policy of compulsory repatriation, if it were to win elections. With Tyndall's blessing, in 1995 Griffin joined the BNP.

That year, Griffin took editorship of a quarterly magazine called *The Rune*, published by the BNP's Croydon branch. It was from here that Griffin made his comments about 'well-directed boots and fists'. He also published articles that described the Holocaust as a 'Holohoax' and threatened the demise of the white race unless immigration was reversed. The racist and anti-Semitic material Griffin published in *The Rune* was so extreme that it led to a police raid on his home, when he was charged under the Public Order Act with for 'publishing or distributing racially inflammatory written material'.

In 1996, Tyndall appointed Griffin editor of the BNP's official magazine, *Spearhead*. From here, Griffin attacked the 'sickly spiral of moderation' in the party. Rather than pursue electoral success – a quest for 'fool's gold', as he put it[8] – the BNP should devote itself to the 'revisionist struggle', in other words Holocaust denial.[9] He also began work on a pamphlet titled *Who Are the Mind-Benders?* (1997), which listed Jews who held prominent positions in the British media, alleging a conspiracy to provide the public with 'an endless diet of pro-multiracial, pro-homosexual, anti-British trash'.

By this stage, it was becoming clear that Griffin had designs on the BNP leadership. In party circles, he was already being discussed as a possible successor to Tyndall, who was now in his early 60s, while in 1997 he was secretly filmed by undercover journalists from ITV's *The Cook Report*, who recorded him outlining a plan to overthrow Tyndall and merge the BNP with what remained of the National Front. But momentum now lay with those 'modernizers' who wanted to tone town the BNP's public image. Under pressure from Butler, Tyndall had been persuaded to stand enough candidates at the 1997 general election to qualify for a party broadcast. The campaign was a dismal failure, costing £60,000 yet averaging only 632 votes per constituency.[10] Butler quit the BNP in frustration, while an ally, Tony Lecomber, remained within the party and launched a magazine, *Patriot*, to challenge Tyndall.

Lecomber's career trajectory is an example of how being an advocate of voter-friendly presentation does not necessarily make one a moderate on the far right. He was the BNP bombmaker who had been sent to prison in 1986. He had served a further term in jail in 1992, for an assault on a Jewish teacher who had tried to remove a BNP sticker outside a tube station in north London. Yet Lecomber, like Butler and several others within the party, came to be convinced that the only way for the BNP to achieve its aim of an all-white Britain was to adopt modern presentational techniques and to build support by winning elections. The glossy, full-colour *Patriot* was used as a showcase for these ideas and by its second issue, published in late 1997, Griffin had phoned Lecomber to tell him he agreed.[11]

Tyndall was not yet aware of it, but his new ally had suddenly become a threat.

This developing split in the BNP did not indicate any great disagreement over party doctrine. Both sides – Tyndall, and the faction that now opposed him – were racial nationalists, who believed that non-white immigration was destroying Britain and had to be reversed. Anti-Semitism and an opposition to 'globalism' circulated freely on both sides, while activists all had well-established track records of involvement in fascist movements. Where they differed, however, was in how their ideas might best be presented to the public.

Tyndall, although he had at times made half-hearted nods towards electoral politics, represented the traditional approach of 'march and grow'. His strategy was to build a street movement (composed of the 'solid types' to whom he had alluded when the BNP was founded in the early 80s), which would eventually be able to bully its way into power, much as Mussolini or Hitler's parties had done before the Second World War. The opposing approach involved using elections as a kind of 'ladder strategy', which would win support at local, then national level, influencing the terms of political debate while at the same time preparing to seize power when the opportune moment arose. To take the latter route would not mean that your party's core beliefs had changed; rather that a second, public-facing discourse would need to be developed, one that concealed the more extreme elements of your doctrine.

In the mid-90s, BNP activists only had to look across the Channel to France to see how this might be done. Under the leadership of Jean-Marie Le Pen, a former paratrooper, the Front National had emerged as a serious force in French politics, winning seats in both local and national government, and receiving 14 per cent of the vote in the 1988 presidential election. Its presence on the political scene helped ensure that immigration remained a contentious political issue, long after the primary flow of migrants to France had all but stopped. This had been achieved largely by following the ideas of the *Nouvelle Droite* – the group of right-wing intellectuals who drew on the ideas of Gramsci and argued that a movement must push for cultural hegemony before it could attain political power.

In pursuit of this hegemony, the Front National had made two key innovations. One was to establish a network of cultural 'circles': associations for war veterans, farmers, women and other social groups that would spread the party's influence beyond its usual limits. The other was to moderate the FN's public language. A bulletin from the party's national training institute stated: 'To appeal to people we must first of all avoid making them afraid and creating a feeling of repulsion . . . You can argue the same thing with as much vigour in a language which is measured and accepted by the public at large.'[12]

With the guidance of Bruno Megret, a key Front National strategist, the party's language was recast in the mould of identity politics. Megret argued that the old distinctions of left and right no longer mattered, and that the true conflict of the post-Cold War era was 'between nationalism and cosmopolitanism, between identity and internationalism.'[13] The intention was to create a 'dual discourse':[14] a respectable language for public consumption, laden with enough hints to signal to the inner circle of activists that the party still held true to its underlying fascist doctrine.

Griffin had dabbled once before with the ideas of the *Nouvelle Droite* during his National Front days. Now, as editor of

Spearhead, and newly promoted to the role of publicity direc-tor, he was well placed to advocate them within the BNP. 'An embryonic Front National exists in Britain,' he promised in February 1998, proposing a new language in which the BNP could present its ideas. This, Griffin explained, boiled down to four key concepts:

Freedom – from the EU, from the tyranny of international finance, and from puppet-status under Washington.

Security – from crime and social collapse, and from the unem-ployment, low pay and economic uncertainty created by globalism.

Democracy – in the sense that the government of Britain should respond to the will of the British people, rather than to the whims of a self-chosen, self-serving politico-media 'elite'.

Identity – the recognition that the artificially-imposed multi-cultural experiment has not worked, that it threatens the very survival of the traditional cultural and ethnic identity of the native people of the British Isles, and that the trends of the last few decades must be reversed if our people are to have a future in their own land.[15]

During this period Griffin struck up an association with Mark Deavin, who shared his enthusiasm for the Front National. Deavin was a former student of the right-wing UK Independence Party's founder Alan Sked, a professor at the London School of Economics. He sat on UKIP's governing executive until his BNP connections were discovered and he was expelled. Invited by Griffin to write for *Spearhead*, Deavin advocated an 'umbrella' alliance of far-right parties that would adopt the communication strategy of the Front National.

Deavin was impressed by the Front National's success in playing down accusations of racism, which he claimed had been achieved with techniques inspired by the pseudo-science of neuro-linguistic programming. 'By employing a sophisticated form of political language semantics,' he wrote, 'the FN has been highly successful in throwing derogatory labels back in the faces of its opponents.' According to Deavin, neuro-linguistic programming held that 'successful communication is best achieved through gently "aligning" an opposing viewpoint with that of your own by finding points of agreement, and then gradually "leading" the other viewpoint around to your position.' To that end, the Front National had 'shaped its communication strategy in a manner which, where and when possible, produces the least amount of resistance in ordinary people.'[16]

Griffin agreed: 'Internally, we need to provide a sense of belonging to something very special, but ordinary electors should see us as just another choice on the political scene.'[17] Hand in hand with this new strategy, he explained, would come an 'alternative media' through which the BNP could preach its message directly to the public. In his role as publicity director, Griffin oversaw a revamp of the BNP website, and established a Media Monitoring Unit, through which activists were encouraged to complain to the press and broadcasters about 'derogatory' references to the BNP. Deavin noted how similar efforts by the BNP's press officer, Michael Newland, had already seen some media outlets begin describing the party as 'far right' or 'ultra-nationalist', rather than 'fascist' or 'Nazi'.[18]

In June 1998, Griffin was given the opportunity to put some

of these ideas about presentation into practice at his trial for the articles he had published in *The Rune*. His plan was to turn the event into a media circus: Osiris Akkebala, a black separatist from Florida, was invited to testify in Griffin's defence. Before Akkebala arrived in the country, BNP activists phoned *The Voice* and *New Nation*, British newspapers aimed at Afro-Caribbean readers. When *New Nation* ran the story, alongside a photograph of Akkebala dressed in a colourful West African dashiki, Griffin's team made thirty copies of the article and posted them to national newspapers; the *Sunday Telegraph* picked up the story.[19] Griffin was found guilty and given a suspended sentence, but his media manipulation had, for a brief moment, put multiracial society in the dock. As Akkebala told the court, 'it is not offensive to me as a black man to hear a white man indicate his proudness about his race. I think that is just a natural state of mind to be in.'[20]

Accompanying the new presentational techniques was a strategy for how the BNP could insinuate itself into local politics. As Deavin described it, 'the whole concept of "community politics" . . . must involve the BNP taking a counter-power approach.' This approach would involve 'helping local residents to pressure council officials; circulating videos to electors; getting nationalist music into the CD players, tape recorders and heads of teenagers; setting up fruit and vegetable delivery rounds to housewives; running taxi services for OAPs and women; setting up football teams and arranging outings for neglected youngsters; and so on . . . carried out in tandem with political work designed to sink roots in target wards.'[21]

Here, then, was a blueprint for how a new-look BNP might operate. But was it a political party, or some sort of confidence trick? 'Of course,' Griffin noted, 'the noble crusade to preserve our race and nation is something very different from the psycho-suicide of the "religious" cult, and we have neither the need nor the inclination to brainwash anybody.'[22]

In November 1998, Griffin made his most open challenge to Tyndall yet, attacking 'extremism' within the party and arguing that the commitment to compulsory repatriation of non-white immigrants should be dropped. Instead, he argued, the BNP should pursue a policy of voluntary repatriation, to be carried out 'over three terms of government'. Yet while Griffin may have had new ideas about how to present the party's message, the BNP's internal doctrine remained as racist as it ever was. Griffin was in politics, he claimed, 'to help stop the immigration which is destroying this and every other white nation in the world . . . I want to see Britain become the 99 per cent genetically white country she was just eleven years before I was born, and I want to die knowing that I have helped to set her on a course whereby her future genetic make-up will one day not even resemble that of January 1948, but that of July 1914.'[23]

Tyndall did not watch these developments without complaint. 'Concern with presenting the right image is not a new phenomenon,' he complained to readers of *Spearhead*. In characteristically verbose style, he attacked 'well-meaning and usually though not always young, people in the nationalist fraternity sounding off as if the BNP had never heard of the arts and crafts of good image-projection before the likes of themselves came along and shone the torch which guided us out of the caves.'[24]

But by early 1999, Griffin had decided to challenge Tyndall for leadership of the BNP. A visit to the Front National's headquarters near Paris shortly after the *Rune* trial had convinced

Griffin that the party needed a more professional form of organization, particularly if it was to fight that year's European Parliament elections. A major obstacle to small parties gaining a foothold in British politics has been the use of 'first past the post' voting – but these elections, to be held in June, would be the first in the UK to use a system of proportional representation. What's more, conditions looked favourable for right-wing parties: the Tories were in disarray, following their landslide election defeat in 1997, while a rural backlash against the Blair Government was in full swing. Hoping to capitalize on this, Griffin had already launched the farming 'circle' Land and People, an imitation of the social clubs through which the Front National had spread its ideas.

In February 1999, prompted by a suspicion that Tyndall was about to alter the party constitution to shore up his leadership, Griffin announced a formal challenge. This meant, as Griffin wrote in a letter to Tyndall, that the forthcoming European campaign would be 'part of our own respective personal campaigns for the leadership contest'. This open competition, Griffin assured, would be 'of positive benefit to the party'.[25]

The election campaign itself, aimed at disaffected Tories who had drifted towards UKIP and James Goldsmith's anti-EU Referendum Party, was a total failure. Despite glossy election publicity designed by Griffin, which bore family-friendly photos and the key terms 'freedom', 'security', 'identity', 'democracy', the party only attracted one per cent of the vote and recruited only a few hundred extra members. UKIP proved the biggest attraction for ex-Tory voters, while the attempt to present a non-threatening image was ruined in May 1999, a month before the election, when nail bombs were planted in the London districts of Brixton, Brick Lane and Soho. It emerged that the bomber, a neo-Nazi named David Copeland who targeted black, Asian and gay Londoners, had previously been a member of the BNP.[26]

Although Griffin had been in charge of campaign strategy, it was Tyndall who took the blame. From the pages of *Spearhead*, Tyndall railed against the 'vicious and divisive conflict' provoked, he claimed, by the modernizers. 'Nick Griffin, not content with utilizing his talents to help promote and build the party as he has done over the past three years, is absolutely determined to take it over and be leader.'[27]

By July, Tyndall had sacked Griffin from his position at *Spearhead*. In response Griffin campaigned for the leadership via the pages of Tony Lecomber's *Patriot*, which presented him as the face of a voter-friendly, modern BNP. His photograph was featured on the cover of one issue accompanied by the slogan 'New Millennium New Leader', while *Patriot* also produced a glossy brochure with the optimistic title 'Moving On, Moving Up', which featured endorsements of Griffin's candidacy from senior party activists.[28] In response, Tyndall issued dire warnings about Griffin's trustworthiness. The September 1999 issue of *Spearhead* featured a statement from Griffin's former Political Soldier associates in the International Third Position: 'In terms of policy and ideology he is inconsistent. He has been a conservative, a revolutionary nationalist, a radical National Socialist, a Third Positionist, a friend of "boot boys" and the skinhead scene, a man committed to respectable politics and electioneering, a "modernizer". Which is he in reality?'[29]

For the time being, most BNP members were willing to overlook that question. At the end of September, the result was announced: Griffin had won, with 1,082 votes to Tyndall's 411. With a turnout of 80 per cent of the party's membership, this was a resounding victory, leaving Tyndall no choice but to concede defeat.[30] He pledged not to be disruptive, and to continue in the BNP as 'an ordinary member', telling his supporters that 'we have all got to pull together in the greater cause of race and nation'.[31]

If losing control of the party he had founded wasn't humiliation enough for Tyndall, by December Griffin had removed his pride and joy, *Spearhead*, from the information packs sent out to interested members of the public. Activists were told to 'forget the ideas for a few minutes and think purely about selling them'.[32] The promise was, to use a phrase popular with other political modernizers of the era: things can only get better.

PART II

5

The Most Tolerant Race on Earth?

As political visions went, it was strikingly banal: 'We want our own way of life back. We want Sunday afternoons, you know, the fellas having a drink at the pub and then coming back home to a Sunday lunch, not twenty-four-hour shopping and corner shops open until ten at night.' But that was exactly the point. The speaker, Sharron Edwards, a fair-haired, presentable mother of three from the West Midlands, was filmed for a BNP promotional video sitting down to dinner with her husband Steve at their house in the Black Country village of Wombourne. This professional couple with their two young children was a rare commodity on the far right: as one veteran activist had complained to me, 'you get a lot of weirdos in fringe politics'.

Edwards did not fit the stereotype of a BNP activist,[1] but she argued that she was far from 'another passenger on the feminist bandwagon'. Women had 'a maternal duty, a natural human capacity to nurture and care for our family under even the most desperate circumstances', and they represented 'the true spirit of nationalism and patriotism – an invaluable commodity when it comes to enlightening those who have been indoctrinated with multi-culturalism, or to bringing up the next generation with healthy values.'[2]

For a brief period at the turn of the millennium Edwards was the face of Nick Griffin's 'modern' BNP. She and her husband were former members of the National Democrats, an offshoot of the conservative wing of the National Front, who had joined the BNP in 1998, encouraged by talk of modernizing the party's image. In his role as publicity director, Griffin had already used the couple on leaflets for the 1999 European election campaign. The same year, Sharron was placed in charge of the family 'circle' Renaissance, another social club in the mould of the French Front National. After he deposed Tyndall, Griffin appointed Sharron deputy chairman, replacing the long-serving Richard Edmonds. Other 'modernizers' were promoted, too: Tony Lecomber was made 'director of group development' and the party's press officer, Michael Newland, was promoted to the newly created role of national treasurer. To give the impression that his leadership would be less autocratic than that of Tyndall, Griffin set up an advisory council composed of senior officials and regional organizers, that was supposed to act as a party 'think tank'; nonetheless, tight control of decision-making remained in the hands of the chairman.[3]

While these internal changes were intended to give the BNP a new air of professionalism, externally, the party's propaganda was transformed. The task was to attract a new layer of supporters who did not necessarily share the party's hardline doctrine while retaining the allegiance of existing activists who did.[4] Griffin's aim was to create a movement that transcended class boundaries. 'It is at this point,' he told his party, 'when the British National Party suddenly becomes the focus of the hopes not just of the neglected and oppressed white working class, but also of the frustrated and disorientated traditional middle class that our future lies.'[5] But to achieve this, the BNP's public language had to change, as Griffin explained to members:

> Emotive words, however justified they may be, must be avoided. Truth hurts, so words like 'alien', 'vermin', 'gang' instead of 'group', and such like must be avoided. A white rapist may be described as a 'beast' or an 'animal', but a black one must merely be a 'criminal' . . . we can get away with criticising Zionists, but any criticism of Jews is likely to be legal and political suicide.[6]

Publicity material was rewritten to centre on the 'four key concepts' of freedom, democracy, security and identity, which Griffin had set out under Tyndall's leadership.[7] Britain under threat was the overriding message – from the corrupt 'LibLabCon' political elite; from the clutches of undemocratic 'Federal Europe'; but most of all from immigration. 'It's not a question of race, it's a question of space,' claimed one frequently distributed leaflet. As always, the solution was to 'restore' Britain's all-white ethnic make-up. But the policy of forced repatriation had been dropped, in favour of encouraging 'family-friendly tax policies to encourage our own people to have more children, and provide generous Homeward Bound grants to the many immigrants who would go home if they could afford to'. What's more, the definition of racism had been turned on its head: in opposing immigration, the party was 'resisting the racist colonisation of Britain in which the native people of Britain are having their culture suppressed, their land colonised and are being discriminated against on racial grounds'.[8]

Curious members of the public who sent off for a copy of the new BNP magazine *Identity*, or visited the revamped website, would quickly be introduced to some rather more familiar themes. The party claimed to be committed to 'modern, populist nationalism' but readers would soon discover that mass immigration was a plot aiming for 'the extinction of the White Man'.[9] What was needed, as Griffin wrote, was nothing less than a 'revolution' that would sweep away the old political elites who had conspired to undermine racial purity. 'The only thing which can save everything we hold dear is total change at all levels of society; in a word, a revolution . . . Nothing less can save our race and nation.'[10]

Why was this information being hidden from the British people? Because, Griffin explained, the media was run by a foreign clique: 'Part of the reason for this huge divide between British popular taste and the enthusiasms of the elite is that a very significant proportion of the latter are not British, either by origin or sentiment. In connection with the mass media, this phenomenon has been well-documented recently in the BNP's publication *The Mind Benders*, and the situation is very similar in other national institutions such as entertainment and the law.'[11]

Despite the surface change, the inner doctrine was the same as ever: a belief in 'revolutionary' seizure of power at a moment of crisis; biological racism; a barely concealed conspiracy theory. But this language of 'identity' was something new. White Britons were discriminated against in their own country, the BNP argued. How, and by whom? And why would anyone believe that this were true?

In 1999, the year Nick Griffin took over the BNP, one organization devoted considerable effort to counter-attacking what it saw as an assault on white Britain. The country, it contended, was in the grip of 'institutionalized idiocy', promoted by a 'new Establishment' composed of an influential liberal elite who were behaving like a 'lynch mob', driven by 'colonial guilt' and 'town hall political correctness', churning out 'sub-Marxist . . . propaganda for the race relations industry'. That organization was the *Telegraph* newspaper, a respected broadsheet. Under the editorship of Charles Moore, it was leading the charge against Sir William Macpherson's report on police failures in solving the murder of Stephen Lawrence.

Lawrence was the black teenager who had been murdered by a group of white youths – one of whom shouted 'nigger' shortly before the crime was committed – at a bus stop in south London in April 1993, not far from the BNP's Welling headquarters. Police had bungled the investigation during its crucial early stages, failing to follow up on leads, showing reluctance to treat the crime as racist, and behaving insensitively towards Lawrence's parents, who felt they were being treated like 'uppity' blacks when they complained about the lack of progress in catching the killers. With the suspects still at large, a campaign for justice was launched by Stephen's parents that even the right-wing *Daily Mail* came to support, and a public inquiry into the case was finally ordered by the Labour Home Secretary Jack Straw, four years after the murder. Macpherson's conclusion – that the Lawrences were victims of 'institutional racism' – was a transformative moment for British society.

For black people, it was official confirmation of what they already knew: that the system worked against them. For many whites, as the journalist Brian Cathcart notes in *The Case of Stephen Lawrence*, it was the first time that they had been invited to see black immigrants and their descendants not as a problem community but as the victims of 'a terrible and tragic injustice'.

As Straw told parliament, the inquiry 'opened all our eyes to what it is to be black or Asian in Britain today'. Thanks to their tireless campaign, the Lawrences were celebrated in official culture: Stephen's parents, Doreen and Neville, were invited to give the Channel 4 alternative Christmas message; ITV screened a two-hour drama based on the family's story; and the artist Chris Ofili won the 1998 Turner Prize for his paintings, one of which was a portrait of Doreen.

All this pointed to a simple fact: by the late 90s, it was abundantly clear that post-war immigrants could no longer be regarded as visitors. Two-thirds of Caribbeans, a third of Chinese residents and the majority of children born in every minority community were born in Britain. And people were mixing: according to a 1997 report by the Policy Studies Institute, among those born in Britain a half of Caribbean men, a third of Caribbean woman and a fifth of Asian men had a white partner.[12]

What's more, since 1997 the New Labour Government had presided over, in the words of the commentator on race relations Gary Younge, a general 'acceptance of diversity' that had not existed under the Conservatives. As Younge told me, 'A lot had changed in the racial conversation and Labour were taking the top off the pressure cooker. Between '97 and 2001, Chris Ofili wins the Turner Prize, Steve McQueen wins the Turner, *White Teeth* comes out, *Goodness Gracious Me* is broadcast. It's not that New Labour does this but it's almost like a Renaissance period of artistic and non-white engagement.'

Race had not played a major part in New Labour's initial pitch to the electorate – indeed, the only non-white face to feature in the 1997 manifesto for a 'New Britain' was that of Nelson Mandela – but the image of a young, diverse Britain fit neatly into Tony

Blair's ambition 'to liberate Britain from the old class divisions, old structures, old prejudices, old ways of working and doing things that will not do in this world of change.'[13]

But this 'pressure cooker' moment was met with unease in some quarters. As Younge said, 'With Macpherson you had people stepping over one another to describe themselves as racist. You had this urgent pent-up new language of race, but you also have this large group of white people who are like, did I miss something? It's a conversation we hadn't had in eighteen years. It's like you just discovered sex but with no foreplay. Quite a confusing moment.'

The Lawrence inquiry, and the debate that followed the publication of Macpherson's report in February 1999, revealed much about Britain's muddled discussion of race at the end of the 90s. The inquiry itself had revealed a shockingly poor understanding of racism among police officers: according to one experienced detective who appeared before the inquiry, racism was simply a matter of 'people making derogatory remarks about people of a different colour'.[14] Likewise, the right-wing press, which had been happy to condemn racism as long as it was confined to the snarling form of the five Lawrence murder suspects ('scum', as they were declared by the *Mail*), utterly rejected the suggestion that respectable Middle England could be complicit in racism too. When Blair gave an interview to the black newspaper *New Nation* in which he claimed Britain was more racist than the US, it sent the *Sun*'s star columnist Richard Littlejohn into paroxysms of rage. Blair's offence was to denigrate that most cherished of national myths – that 'the British, particularly the English, are the most tolerant race on earth'. Especially so, Littlejohn argued, since 'no-one ever voted for a multi-cultural society. It was imposed upon them.'[15]

The backlash came from the top of the establishment downwards. The *Telegraph*'s editor Charles Moore argued that Macpherson 'imposes on his victims, the police, a concept of racism that makes them guilty whatever they do'. The Police Federation, which represented rank and file officers, was also critical, claiming that the report accused individual police officers of being racist (it didn't) and that it would damage morale. The Tory leader William Hague was later to argue that it had led to a rise in street crime. For others, the affair was yet more evidence of Britain's decline. 'It was never thus in the old days,' complained the former *Sunday Telegraph* editor Peregrine Worsthorne. 'A man walked taller because he was British; held his head higher. To be born British was . . . a kind of grace or blessing, a mark of God's favour.' Borrowing from Enoch Powell, he declared: 'Nations which the gods wish to destroy, they first drive mad, and this does indeed seem to be Britain's fate.' The Conservative MP Humfrey Malins darkly prophesied that 'the silent, law-abiding majority will soon come to resent enforced political correctness and will not stand idly by.' Macpherson, no crusading liberal, but a deeply establishment figure, eventually had to stop giving media interviews, such was the volume of hate mail he received.

It was in the murkier waters of this much larger pool of white resentment that the BNP constructed its propaganda. A focus on white victims of 'racist' crime would become a staple feature of publicity material, accompanied by the slogan 'Racism Cuts Both Ways'; Griffin later denigrated Stephen Lawrence as a 'drug dealer'. One cartoon, circulated by the BNP in the early 2000s, showed the Met commissioner Sir Paul Condon receiving an 'eye test' in which the name Stephen Lawrence was printed large, followed by the almost illegible names of white victims of crime. Another leaflet copied a Metropolitan Police press advert that bore the slogan 'race crime is hate crime' and subverted the message to imply that white victims were being deliberately overlooked.[16] Exploiting white fears of black crime had been a feature of far-right propaganda since the tabloid-driven 'mugging' panic of the 1970s, if not earlier, but this pushed the rhetoric further, absorbing and then twisting the logic of anti-racism. The Rights for Whites campaign of the early 90s had been expanded into a dominant propaganda theme.

Even as debate raged over whether or not Britain was a racist country, a new scapegoat was on the rise. In his diary entry for 14 September 1999, the Labour MP Chris Mullin recalls a memo, sent by the Home Secretary Jack Straw to the prime minister's office, expressing alarm at the 'unprecedented' numbers of asylum applications received by the UK that year. At around 70,000, it was a relatively small number, yet Mullin gloomily recorded, 'Fortress Europe is disintegrating. If this goes on, will we need a new Berlin wall to protect the fortunate from the depredations of the destitute? Will Europe be overwhelmed in the end? As Rome was by the barbarians.'[17]

Britain, like every country that signed up to the Geneva Convention, had an obligation to accept refugees. The modern stigma attached to them began in the 1980s when large number of young men fled the civil war in Sri Lanka, at precisely the time the Thatcher Government was trying to keep South Asian immigrants from 'swamping' Britain.[18] During the 1990s, a growing official culture of suspicion over asylum and the result-ing delays in processing applications left the system struggling to cope. When Labour came to power in 1997 it tried to solve the problem by introducing a computerized system and dispersing asylum-seekers around the country rather than allowing them to congregate in London and other large cities.

The policy was a disaster: the computer system did not work properly and dispersal left refugees isolated from the networks of community support that existed in cities where their compatriots had settled. Instead they were sent to live in towns that had neither the infrastructure nor the expertise to cope with their arrival. Local newspapers fanned the flames of hostility, with one particularly noxious editorial in the *Dover Express* likening 750 mainly Roma gypsies who had been settled in the town to 'human sewage'. This in turn was picked up by the national press, especially the *Daily Mail*, which turned the asylum-seeker into a modern folk devil with headlines such as 'brutal crimes of the asylum seekers'; 'the good life on asylum alley'; or 'suburbia's little Somalia'.[19] Conveniently, given that many (but not all) asylum-seekers came from Eastern or Central Europe, the press was able to pursue racist stereotyping – obsessively linking asylum-seekers with crime and disease; describing them in dehumanizing terms as a 'flood' or a 'horde' – while sidestepping the accusation of anti-black racism.

To compound the problem, the press systematically confused refugees with economic migrants – people entering Britain, legally or illegally, to find work on farms, or in the fast-growing service industries of the South East. The 'flexible' labour market championed by Thatcher and continued under New Labour demanded a ready supply of low-paid workers, yet they too were met with hostility. Lumped together under the stereotype of the 'bogus' asylum-seeker, immigrants were accused of entering the country simply to claim benefits or use public services.

'They couldn't find my granny a bed but they open the wards

for gipsies', read one particularly toxic *Mail* headline.[20] Anti-asylum-seeker rhetoric also fit neatly with the image of the benefits 'scrounger'; as the *Mirror* columnist Tony Parsons wrote, previous immigrants 'gained acceptance by working harder than the locals. That's why the rash of baby-toting Romanian beggars rubs the nation up the wrong way. Britain became a successful multi-racial country because the newcomers were ready to graft.'[21] Scarce resources in hospitals and other public services were a consequence of the 'modernity' to which New Labour had so enthusiastically signed up, yet nobody in government seemed willing to defend or even explain that. Instead, asylum-seekers made a convenient scapegoat for a creaking welfare state.

Herman Ouseley, who was chair of the Commission for Racial Equality from 1993 to 2000, told me that he warned Straw about press coverage of asylum as early as 1997: 'I said the most important thing you have to do when it comes to race relations is to counter the misinformation about asylum, about refugees, because that is doing enormous damage in the way in which people are taking that information and turning it around into hateful, resentful positions.'

Ouseley suggested the government launch a public information campaign to disseminate accurate information about immigration and asylum, but Straw was unwilling to listen: 'Jack's reaction to me was, we have a free press, we have free expression and we can't tell the press what to do.'[22]

Instead, the distorted portrayals of asylum-seekers were allowed to corrode public attitudes. A survey carried out for *Reader's Digest* by Ipsos Mori in 2000 found that people consistently overestimated the scale of immigration: Respondents estimated on average that around 20 per cent of the population were immigrants (in reality, it was 4 per cent). They also estimated that asylum-seekers received on average £113 a week in benefits (the reality was £36.54 a week, of which only £10 could be spent freely). More worryingly, while respondents displayed overwhelmingly positive attitudes to black and Asian minorities, the number of people who thought Britain was becoming a more racially prejudiced country was on the rise for the first time since the 1980s.[23]

The BNP targeted its campaigns at precisely this fault line, where anxiety at immigration crossed paths with anxiety at the failings of the welfare state. A commonly distributed leaflet asked 'Asylum seekers? Longer hospital waiting lists? More wage cuts? More homelessness? Enough is enough!' The leaflet demanded that 'local councils should start putting native-born British people to the front of the housing queue for a change.'[24]

Yet for the time being the BNP remained on the sidelines. It was the Tories who made asylum a prominent election issue. In the spring of 2000, as local elections approached, William Hague was desperately seeking a way to shore up his foundering leadership of the Conservative Party. The right-wing press was on hand with suggestions: On 15 March the *Sun* criticized 'timid' William for the Tories' failure to launch a campaign 'against beggars and fake asylum-seekers'. Hague should not fear being branded 'jingoistic, nationalistic or racist'. The *Telegraph* columnist Janet Daley suggested that an attack on the consensus over race and immigration could be the 'big idea' that Hague needed to challenge Labour at the next general election.[25]

The next month, in a speech to the Social Market Foundation, Hague made immigration an election issue for the first time since 1979, when he criticized the government for allowing a 'massive influx of bogus asylum-seekers'. Shortly afterwards, his deputy Ann Widdecombe proposed that all asylum-seekers be detained on arrival in the UK. Labour responded by trying to out-tough the Tories. The Home Office minister Barbara Roche attacked Roma beggars on the London Underground: 'These people have come here with the intention of exploiting the system and exploiting their children. It's a vile thing to do.' On 11 April, a spokesperson for Tony Blair said: 'If you take Kosovo out of the equation, then, on the latest evidence, around 70 to 80 per cent of asylum-seekers' cases are not genuine.' As the *Sun* responded, 'The majority ARE bogus – the Prime Minister has said as much.'[26]

In this atmosphere, the BNP saw the first signs of electoral growth. Its treasurer Michael Newland, a building contractor from Kentish Town and an articulate media operator with a respectable image, was selected to run as candidate for London mayor in May. His election address, co-written by Griffin, devoted considerable space to 'bogus' asylum-seekers, wrapped up in the party's repackaged racism: 'Opposition to immigration is not a matter of "racism" or "hate" against other peoples. What we oppose is the destruction of the tradi-tional identity of the British people in our homeland . . . We ask for our culture, freedoms and our traditions to be respected, and for the majority to have the right to run our country as they wish.' A BNP mayor, said the manifesto, would stop 'politically correct diversity policing', 'multicultural indoctri-nation' in education and reject positive discrimination for public appointments because 'it is patronising, and racist against whites'. Newland attracted 33,569 first-preference votes and 45,337 second-preference votes.[27]

In July, the party came second in a council by-election in

Bexley, south-east London: its best result since 1993. Although only 390 asylum-seekers were housed in the borough as a whole – the third-lowest total in London – the BNP successfully exploited fears among residents of the borough's deprived North End ward, with leaflets that claimed it had become a 'dumping ground' for asylum-seekers and that immigrants 'milk the benefit system' while 'British children are in poverty'. These claims bore a resemblance to those of the local Tories, who claimed Britain was 'the biggest soft touch in the world' for bogus asylum-seekers, while after the election, Nigel Beard, the local Labour MP, appeared to endorse the myth that asylum-seekers were responsible for the poverty of his own constituents: 'I walk into pubs and people shout, "when are you going to do something for the English?" That is not racist. It is a feeling of being bypassed, left in the queue for services while others go to the front. The area is almost exclusively white working class. It is an understandable reaction.' The campaign was accompanied by reports of attacks and abuse directed at the seventeen asylum-seeker families who actually lived in the ward.[28]

Tony Blair would later argue that it was 'precisely to reduce racism' that his government took a 'tough' approach to asylum.[29] Griffin spun a different line. 'It's been quite fun to watch government ministers and the Tories play the race card in far cruder terms than we would ever use, but pretend not to. This issue legitimises us.'[30] He was exaggerating for effect, and the BNP's progress was minute. Its resources were limited and what small progress it made was clearly dependent on its ability to mobilize activists in a particular area – which at this stage appeared to be a small corner of the West Midlands and London's outer fringes. But it now had a language in which to clothe its racism and a target on which to focus – both of which were shared by sections of the political mainstream.

The election results in May and July 2000 suggested there was potential, however limited, for the repackaged BNP, but by August, Griffin's leadership had run into serious trouble. That month marked the inaugural Red White and Blue festival, an expanded version of a 'family day' that Sharron Edwards had organized in 1999. Here, cheerful activities such as a football tournament and stalls offering candy-floss and face-painting would be mixed with racist literature, recordings of anti-Semitic speeches and a rally, at which Griffin and other senior figures would preach racial purity.[31] The occasion should have been a chance for Griffin to show the party faithful that his strategy was bearing fruit but instead it was marked by discord: Griffin had sacked Michael Newland from his post as treasurer a week earlier, while Sharron Edwards did not even turn up, having been told by Griffin that she would be out of the party by the end of the year.

The immediate cause of conflict was money. In the summer of 2000, Michael Newland and Sharron Edwards questioned Griffin's use of party finances, along with a second-hand car business 'run by a co-operative of British National Party members and supporters' that was advertised in the party newspaper. Griffin issued a members' bulletin that claimed the pair were trying to destabilize the party and sacked Newland.[32]

On 30 July, Sharron Edwards sent a letter to BNP members that included a petition in support of Newland. Over the August bank holiday weekend, Newland and Edwards were summoned to a meeting of the Advisory Council. Newland was suspended from the party for 'spreading deliberately misleading and inaccurate accounting records' and Edwards was expelled for having circulated the petition. Her husband was also expelled for 'encouraging a boycott of the Red, White and Blue festival'.[33]

This move failed to quell dissent. Many BNP activists, particularly those in the West Midlands who had followed the Edwards into the BNP from the National Democrats, were outraged at the dismissal of their fellow activists. In October, Griffin and Lecomber were forced to attend a fractious meeting of the West Midlands BNP at a leisure centre in Tipton. Amid jeers from the audience and heckles of 'he's lying just like Tony Blair', Griffin and Lecomber were forced to back down and readmit the expelled members.[34]

The episode was part of a wider tension that ran deeper than a mere personality clash. Even as Griffin and Lecomber fell into conflict with their fellow 'modernizers', there were signs that the hardline membership was not happy with the direction the party had been taking. Tyndall, who had maintained relative silence during the first few months of Griffin's leadership, was beginning to agitate against him. His criticism grew louder when Griffin attempted to take the BNP's 'non-racist' image a step further by establishing an 'ethnic liaison committee'. Nominally staffed by three BNP activists, one of whom was the half-Turkish Leon Rustem – who claimed to have joined the party after he was mugged by black teenagers in East London[35] – the 'committee' was a propaganda tool. But as Tyndall warned BNP members, it was 'the thin end of the wedge of admission of non-whites to the party'.[36]

When Griffin removed Sharron Edwards as candidate for a parliamentary by-election in West Bromwich West in the autumn of 2000 and imposed himself in her place, it provoked a split. Local activists refused to canvass for Griffin, while the Edwards joined with Eddy Butler – who had left the BNP in 1996 – to form the Freedom Party. Here, they were able to try out anti-immigrant politics without the neo-Nazi baggage, and Sharron Edwards went on to win a seat on Staffordshire borough council in May 2003. Griffin had alienated his modernizing allies, and he was now facing growing dissent from the party hard core.

The year 2000 may have been a make-or-break moment for the BNP, but the country too was at 'a turning point, a crossroads', as a major report on race relations published that October warned. The Commission on the Future of Multi-Ethnic Britain drew together a number of leading thinkers on race, who concluded that the country was faced with a choice. With careful guidance, Britain could become a 'community of communities . . . at ease with its place in world society and with its own internal differences'. But the opportunity was 'in danger of being squandered': rising tensions, such as the moral panic over asylum-seekers, could leave the country divided, a place full of hostility and resentment. The Commission called on the government to make a formal declaration that Britain was a multicultural, multi-faith society.[37]

This was supposed to herald the next big step in New Labour's race relations agenda. After the Macpherson inquiry, and the amendment to the Race Relations Act that followed, compelling a range of public bodies to promote good race relations, the government was preparing to throw its weight behind the Commission. With some fanfare, its report was to be launched by the home secretary at a press conference on 11 October.

The weekend before, however, the *Telegraph* got hold of a

seemingly innocuous line in the report which pointed out that for many people, the notion of Britishness held 'largely unspoken' racial connotations – i.e. that many people assumed 'British' meant 'white' – and that a more inclusive national identity should be promoted instead. Again, the 'liberal establishment' was accused of sullying Britain's reputation for tolerance. In the face of this onslaught, the government panicked. At the report's own launch, Jack Straw publicly distanced himself from its findings and said there would be no rethinking of Britishness. 'I do not accept the arguments of those on the nationalist right or the liberal left that Britain as a cohesive whole is dead. I am proud of what I believe to be the best of British values.'[38]

Why such a capitulation? For Bhikhu Parekh, the political theorist who chaired the Commission, it was no surprise. I interviewed Parekh, now a member of the House of Lords, in 2011, and he told me that there had been a pressing need to rethink national identity at the end of the 90s: devolution, further integration with the European Union and the facts of a multicultural society threw the whole idea of 'Britishness' into question. New Labour's response, Parekh said, was paper-thin: 'Tony Blair and others said it's a new Britain, like New Labour. And to them, new Britain meant young Britain. It was pathetic, because young Britain had no appeal at a time when a large population was elderly and retired, and the young people had felt alienated from the mainstream.'

Just as, economically, Labour was offering a version of Thatcherism with some of the rough edges smoothed over, culturally it preferred to stick with 'best of British'. Tony Blair claimed to have held lofty (if vague) ambitions for race relations at the start of his premiership: 'I wanted us to take the good bits of the Labour Party in the 1970s and 80s – proper progressive attitudes such as equality for women, gays, blacks and Asians – and ally them to normality, bring them into the mainstream and out of the suffocating strictures of political correctness.'[39]

But when challenged by the right, Labour backed down. One year later, the BNP would play a crucial and corrosive role in shaping a new politics of race.

6

One Law for Them and Another for Us

On Colne Road, one of the main thoroughfares leading out of Burnley and into the surrounding Lancashire hills, sits an old library building. Its heavy grey stone exterior, a relic of municipal grandeur from Burnley's heyday as a mill town, now houses a community centre staffed by volunteers. As I arrived there late one Thursday afternoon in the summer of 2011, it was closing for the day and a stream of people – white and Asian, young and old – filed past me on their way out. The visitors had been taking lessons in English and maths; burnishing their CVs; doing whatever they could to improve their chances in a job market where the odds were stacked against them. 'This is neutral territory,' the centre's genial manager, Richard Chipps, told me. 'Everyone feels comfortable in here.'

At first sight, it was unremarkable: an image of everyday multicultural Britain, no doubt repeated in towns and cities across the country. But here on Colne Road, which divides the predominantly Asian districts of Daneshouse and Stoneyholme from their largely white neighbours, I was watching a minor miracle. Just a few years previously, Burnley was the scene of the BNP's first electoral breakthroughs under Nick Griffin: the nadir of a series of events that led to the town being branded 'racist capital of Britain'. Chipps, himself a former BNP voter, was one of many Burnley residents determined never to let it happen again. 'I thought, I can't cope with another generation living through these problems,' he told me, explaining why he and Ishtiaq, a Muslim youth worker, had tried hard to make the centre a place where whites and Asians could mix. 'You think about Enoch Powell and you think perhaps his timing were off – perhaps in the future what he said will happen and that it's just going to take longer. Well, this country is too good for that, I don't want it to happen.'

Ten years ago, Colne Road found itself at the centre of a riot. On the night of Friday 22 June 2001, a fight between rival drug dealers – some white, some Asian – broke out in front of a Burnley nightclub. The fighting spread up Colne Road, and several cars were damaged. Later that evening, an Asian taxi driver who stopped to inspect the damaged cars was attacked with a hammer by a group of whites. Thanks to the radio network over which Burnley's mainly Asian taxi drivers communicated, rumours that the driver had died spread quickly through the town. The following evening, a group of Asian men attacked the Duke of York pub on Colne Road; its white customers ran out onto the street with makeshift weapons, before police managed to drive the two groups apart.[1] What had begun as a turf war had now become ethnic conflict.

The Burnley riot was one of a string of 'disturbances', as they are known by official euphemism, to break out across the North of England in the spring and summer of 2001, bringing communities that had been excluded from Labour's New Britain to national attention. In Bradford, then Oldham, then Burnley, then Bradford again, local tensions spilled over into violence between whites and Asians. All three shared the same broad patterns of economic deprivation and racism – and in all three towns the situation was made worse by the BNP and its fellow-travellers on the far right.

It was in Oldham, a satellite of Manchester, where the BNP had seen the greatest potential. As far back as 1998, Griffin had identified Oldham as a target for BNP campaigns. That year a branch was established, surprising party leaders by the rapid take-up.[2] Above all, one issue seemed to be driving BNP support – a perception among some white residents that Asian youths were given an easier ride by police, and that certain parts of the town were 'no-go' areas for whites. The grievances continued to simmer, amplified by the local press. On 3 March 2001, as complaints grew more vocal, the BNP held a Rights for Whites rally outside the police station.[3]

In April, two months before the general election, this was turned into a live political issue when Greater Manchester Police (perhaps still smarting from the accusations of 'institutional racism') drew public attention to an allegedly high level of assaults on whites by Asian youths in Oldham, claims that were picked up by the national press. The next day, the situation worsened when a white pensioner named Walter Chamberlain was beaten up by a group of young Asian men in the town centre. The bruised and battered face of Chamberlain, a D-Day veteran, was pictured on the *Chronicle*'s front page. Now white resentment had its symbolic victim.

At this opportunity, Griffin announced he would stand for parliament in West Oldham. Clearly he would benefit if race relations worsened – and while the BNP had to be seen to distance itself from violent activity, other far-right groups had no such worries. Throughout May, the National Front (a remnant of which had survived largely in England's North West) joined forces with Oldham-based football hooligans and Combat 18 activists, and repeatedly tried to march through Asian-inhabited areas. Griffin tried to ingratiate himself with these groups but the rivalry was vicious and on 26 May, he was chased out of an Oldham pub by Combat 18 activists.[4]

That evening, the far right finally managed to provoke a riot in the Asian-inhabited area of Glodwick. As national media descended on Oldham, Griffin used the opportunity to position himself as the voice of the town's disaffected whites. He was invited on to Radio 4's flagship current affairs programme *Today*, drawing strong criticism from anti-fascists for breaking the BBC's long-standing policy of 'no platform' for fascist politicians. In interviews, Griffin pushed a racist interpretation of events, advocating Northern Ireland-style 'peace walls' to keep communities separate. In keeping with the BNP's new rhetoric, he claimed it was not the Asians' colour that was the problem, it was their culture – specifically their Muslim religion:

> [Muslims are] the biggest problem at present, for several reasons, because they have the highest birth rate, which means their communities need living space – that's what the ethnic cleansing is about. They have political corruption in their own countries, and when they have a chance to get council places they are there for graft. Most important of all is that Islam is an aggressive religion.[5]

At the general election, against a background of widespread apathy (a record low turnout nationally, and down by 18 per cent in the North West), Griffin came third with 16.4 per cent of the vote. He used the night of the count for some further posturing, appearing on the platform with a gag around his mouth and a t-shirt bearing the slogan 'gagged for telling the truth'. It appeared to have the desired effect. As one woman told *The Times*, 'I voted BNP and I don't worry who knows it. Everyone in the street voted for them. This morning I feel like someone is actually fighting for the white people of Oldham, for their rights.'[6]

Fast-forward two weeks, and in Burnley, by the Sunday, tensions were running dangerously high. Again organized racists were on hand to make sure the situation erupted. According to the official police report, customers from the Duke of York had moved up the road to another pub, the Baltic, where a 'minority' were known to 'have nationalist views and travel to Northern Ireland at the time of Loyalist parades'. Drinking outside on a warm Sunday afternoon, a 'siege mentality' developed among the crowd, who began singing 'No surrender to the IRA' and abusing or attacking the Asian drivers of passing cars.

Again, the taxi radio network kicked into action, and by the evening groups of Asian men had gathered in the Daneshouse area off Colne Road to defend their community. Meanwhile, word had spread via a rival network, the mobile phones used by Burnley's white football hooligans, who were gathering in pubs throughout the town.[7] When a group of white men tried to enter Daneshouse, police were only just able to keep the two groups apart, shepherding the whites into the town centre, where they attacked Asian-owned restaurants and taxi offices. Each side retreated into their 'own' community. Asians attacked the working men's club in Daneshouse, and set fire to the Duke of York. This was met with arson attacks on Asian businesses, homes and vehicles in Burnley Wood, a mainly white area.

Residents later reported seeing 'white men who were strangers to the area' driving through and inspecting premises owned by Asians, shortly before they were set on fire.

The next day, a Monday, Nick Griffin came to town with the media in tow. Burnley had taken BNP strategists somewhat by surprise: while they were trying to turn Oldham into the front line of a race war, the party's candidate here – a local man with no media profile – had fared almost as well as Griffin at the general election, coming fourth, with 11 per cent of the vote.

Steven Smith lives in a modest cottage in Cliviger, a small hill-side village on the outskirts of Burnley. Known locally as 'stone wall Smith', this former accountant runs a dry stone walling business – a skill much in demand in the pretty Lancashire countryside. He is also regarded as something of a crank: when I first called, Smith was out, walking the town centre wearing a wooden sandwich board. Immigrants, Islam, 'political correctness' and the town's Asian population are his usual targets – when I managed to contact Smith a few days later, he told me that his current target was a newly-opened deli that had allegedly been serving halal meat without informing its customers. 'He seems a lovely man, ever so polite,' one of Smith's stone wall clients, the owner of a farmhouse near Cliviger, told me. 'But then you see the vitriol of what he writes in his leaflets. You can hardly believe it's the same person.'[8]

When I finally tracked Smith down, he was indeed polite, turning prickly only when I asked if he considered himself a racist: 'That word's only been in circulation for the past twenty or so years and it's just an invention of the left to stop people like me and others complaining about what's happening in the country.'

It's not that he denied being a racist, only that he didn't see anything wrong with it. 'You've got to step outside the box: a racist is basically someone that believes in preserving who and what they are and by bringing tens of thousands if not millions of black and brown people into this country, eventually you're going to finish up with a mongrel race of people. Now I don't think all them boys and girls that fought in two world wars did so for that, and had they seen or known what was going to happen, I doubt very few of them would actually have gone to war.'

Smith had been a presence on Burnley's political scene since the early 90s, when he chained himself to the town hall railings in protest at a twinning project with a village in Pakistan. In another town, at another time, that might have been the highlight of his political career – a bizarre headline in a local newspaper. But in 1999, he set up a branch of the BNP; in 2001 he stood as the party's general election candidate; and in 2002 had helped three candidates win seats on the local council.

The majority of Burnley's voters may not have shared his fears about a 'mongrel race', but something in what Smith had to offer evidently touched a nerve. Visiting the town, a decade on, would I be able to find anybody who could tell me why?

After Wendy Graham, a Burnley community activist, picked me up from the station, the first thing she did was drive me out to Towneley Park, the landscaped grounds of a country house that once belonged to the local aristocratic family. The detour was meant to serve as a gentle warning to a journalist, freshly-arrived from London, not to let their prejudices get the better of them. The day before I arrived, Burnley had made national headlines for boasting Britain's cheapest house – a three-bedroom terrace that sold at auction for £10,000. 'They called

Burnley a run-down former mill town,' she said. 'It makes me see red. Does this look run-down to you?'

Like many others I met, Graham was fiercely proud of her town. But as we drove around the centre, it became clear that Burnley had not benefited from the boom years. Too small and too tucked away in the Pennines to attract the glitzy, property market-driven regeneration schemes of a city like Manchester, its textile mills sit derelict. Now in her fifties, Graham can remember the clatter of the looms, but they fell silent in the 1980s. The area in which they sit has been optimistically rebranded the Weavers' Triangle, but the mills were still waiting to be converted into shops and flats.

In places, it seems as if a slow, silent catastrophe has befallen the town. Whole streets of back-to-back terraces are boarded up, the houses rotting where they stand. Others have been demolished, leaving patches of grass and the ghosts of street patterns. Government money to renovate Burnley's housing stock had been provided since 2003, Graham explained, but the areas earmarked for redevelopment fell victim to property speculators – landlords who bought up scores of vacant houses and demanded extortionate sums of money from the council, or else moved in 'problem' tenants (drug addicts, people evicted from social housing) who were willing to put up with poorly-maintained properties. Graham knew of houses without running water, or where the landlord had laid carpet straight onto a dirt floor.

The longer the houses sit empty, the more they fall prey to arsonists, or to thieves who cannibalize the lead from the roofs, or stone flags from the old scullery floors, which are sold on to wealthy homeowners out in the Lancashire countryside. Often, the theft is brazen: 'They turn up wearing these hi-vis jackets,'

Graham said. 'By the time you've phoned the council to check whether they're genuine, they're gone.'

Some, like Graham, who has lived on the same two streets her whole life, have decided to stay and work to improve their neighbourhood. Many others have moved out to the surrounding villages or further afield. Burnley is one of the few towns in England with a declining population: the number of residents fell by 4.7 per cent between 2001 and 2010, to just over 85,000.[9] It is a town marked by emigration, not immigration – and many residents feel abandoned: 'You feel like you're being kept at arm's length. People do still have a sense of pride in the place, and the BNP appeal to people's sentiment and nostalgia.'

The other thing the BNP appealed to was a feeling, shared by some of the town's white residents, that 'Asian' areas of the town were being favoured with what little public money there was. In 1995, a former Labour councillor named Harry Brooks, then sitting as an independent, gave an interview to the *Burnley Express* in which he claimed the council had been disproportionately allocating funds to Asian community groups for 'political' reasons. The paper gave these claims the front page – the start of a campaign that grew throughout the late 1990s. One example of the newspaper's generous coverage was a feature headlined 'We can't take any more of this squalor', which juxtaposed an image of renovated houses in Daneshouse with dilapidated homes in Burnley Wood. In truth, the 'Asian' areas were receiving the funding because they needed it the most, ranking among the most deprived wards in England. Daneshouse and Stoneyholme were no ghettos: some 40 per cent of the ward's residents were white, but Brooks's campaign racialized Burnley's economic neglect. He directly compared the 'appalling neglect into which some traditionally white working-class areas had been allowed to fall', with the money spent on Daneshouse and Stoneyholme. According to Brooks, this was good reason for 'many decent, non-racist citizens' to abandon Labour, who were 'the only large-scale political outfit in the town'.[10]

But the fact that 'Asian' areas existed at all in Burnley was itself a legacy of racism. During the 1960s and 1970s, workers from Pakistan had been encouraged to come and prop up the region's faltering textile industry. Because of the unsociable hours they were asked to work – often filling vacancies on the night shift – and because of local councils' refusal to house them on the smarter white estates, these immigrants tended to settle in the most run-down parts of town, close to the mills.

When the mills finally closed in the 1980s, these communities were cut off from the economic lifeline that had enabled some of their white forebears to save money and move out to more salubrious parts. Groups of young, unemployed Asian men pooled their resources and started taxi firms or kebab shops: these small economic success stories exacerbated resentment among whites who had lacked the wherewithal to do the same.

There also developed a perception that having Asian neighbours would bring down house prices. Richard Chipps grew up in Rosegrove, a smarter working-class area than Daneshouse and Stoneyholme, and says that Asian shopkeepers who tried to set up businesses in the area were routinely harassed: 'In Rosegrove, they only allowed one Asian shop – and I mean *allowed*. All the others were hounded out because if you let one in you'll let them all in. And they only let him in because they couldn't get a white person to stay open on Sunday evenings.'

Shahid Malik, a former Labour MP who grew up in Daneshouse, described his childhood to me as a 'racist hell on earth'. He continued: 'As we saw white people moving out you'd get some Asian people thinking why don't we try to move out as well, to places like Padiham [a village on the outskirts of Burnley], but when the excrement through the letterbox and the graffiti came they started to move back to the places where they felt most secure.'

At the same time, a younger, British-born generation of Asians were not as willing to put up with the racist abuse experienced by their parents. As Malik explained, 'when I was growing up, the violence was one way, it was racists and it was white on those of Asian origin. That's not how it ended up. And later on you did start to see some indiscriminate racist attacks on white people as well.'

A perception that crime committed by Asians was not taken as seriously bred resentment among the town's whites. 'It's one law for them and another for us,' was how Paul, a white taxi driver put it to me. 'The police are scared to deal with them [Asians] because they'll be called racist,' he said. 'You read all this stuff in the newspapers, you see an Asian lad doing 120 down the M65 and he'll get a six-month driving ban for speeding. Then the next day there'll be a white lad who'll get a twelve-month ban for doing 80.'

Was this 'political correctness' at work? When I asked Chief Inspector Ian Sewart of Lancashire Police, he appeared to agree: 'If you look back there was a time we were afraid of being [perceived as] racist.' He blamed the Macpherson inquiry: 'When a whole organization gets labelled as institutionally racist, culturally that has a big impact.' According to Mike Waite, a senior council manager in charge of community cohesion, the cause of such problems was not so much political as practical: a lack of adequate training meant that council officials 'had an anxiety that they would be called "racist" for taking action – for example to enforce a planning regulation, or a health and safety rule in relation to the taxi trade or a fast food business.' Such failures only encouraged feelings of mutual suspicion between white and Asian inhabitants.

By 2000 Burnley had eleven independent councillors. Led by Harry Brooks, they formed the main opposition to a Labour Party that had long dominated local politics. This group campaigned for the council's translation unit to be closed down, and for funding to be withdrawn from the Bangladesh Welfare Association and other Asian community groups. The effect was to racialize the whole political culture, with other parties moving to compete on the territory carved out by Brooks. In 1996, the Lib Dems were criticized for distributing false information in their campaign material about the funding of Asian voluntary groups; in 1998, the Tories criticized the council for neglecting problems like litter, preferring instead to 'spend ridiculously high amounts of money on *certain areas*' (my italics). Burnley Labour party politics were shaped by this rightward drift: in 1997, there was controversy when a number of its own councillors were investigated and disciplined for pressurizing council officers not to house Asian families in their wards. The local racial equality council had its funding withdrawn by Labour during the late 1990s.[11]

Brooks and his independents did not stand a candidate in the 2001 general election. The BNP's Steven Smith stepped into the gap. His tactics were crude but effective: Smith estimates that he personally delivered 30,000 leaflets to homes before the 2001 election. Smith would attach his notorious sandwich board to a trailer at the back of his car and drive around the town centre.

He sent a stream of letters to the local papers, who were so willing to print them, Smith claims, that he had to invent a range of pseudonyms with which to sign them.[12]

Smith's fourth place in the 2001 general election was enough to establish the BNP as a voice on the town's political scene. Two months after the riot in June 2001, when a government 'task force' descended on Burnley to examine what had gone wrong, the BNP was invited to give an official submission. A letter from the party claimed the riots were 'a direct consequence of the enforced multi-racial society, which nobody wanted nor asked for', blaming 'anti-white race attacks' for triggering the violence and claimed that 'for many years Burnley has suffered at the hands of an out of touch and inept council' that 'continually discriminated' against 'the majority of Burnley council tax payers'.

These views appeared to be shared widely. A 2001 survey representative of Burnley's 45,000 households found that 58 per cent of respondents blamed 'racism by Asian people' for the riots. A similar percentage blamed a lack of mixing among Asian and white people – but, in a sign of mutual hostility, only 18 per cent thought that encouraging more mixing would help.[13]

In the year after the riots, a new national narrative developed: neither economic deprivation nor white racism was seen to be the root cause; rather it was the deficient culture of an Asian Muslim minority. This view appeared to be endorsed by some Labour MPs. In July 2001 after riots broke out in Bradford, provoked by the National Front and exacerbated by Asian anger at the police's failure to protect them, the recently appointed Home Secretary David Blunkett threatened to deploy water cannons and tear gas.

The same month, Ann Cryer, MP for Keighley, near Bradford, suggested that arranged marriages and poor English skills were responsible for Muslims failing to integrate.[14] In December, a series of official reports into the riots was published, chief among them one by Ted Cantle which identified communities' 'parallel lives' as the main cause of unrest. White racism, and the failure of New Labour to set out a vision which could give hope to an industrial working class decimated by Thatcherism, were played down. In just two years, New Labour had gone from 'what it is to be black or Asian in Britain today' to blaming the victims.

The atmosphere of fear and suspicion surrounding British Muslims also intensified after 9/11. With no small irony, Blair himself wrote in his memoirs that 'certain categories' of immigrants, 'from certain often highly troubled parts of the world . . . imported their own internal issues, from those parts of the world, into the towns and villages in Britain.'[15] This gave an opportunity for the BNP to broaden its own propaganda. In the autumn of 2001, the party distributed leaflets that claimed 'Islam' stood for 'Intolerance, Slaughter, Looting, Arson and Molestation of Women'. It also sought to exploit religious divisions among British Asians. Griffin's 'ethnic liaison committee' claimed to have made contact with Sikhs and Hindus, whose contributions were distributed on an audio cassette. As one activist in Burnley subsequently told an undercover journalist, 'We're not interested in chasing Muslim votes so we can actually publicly say . . . we're going to deport them all. If saying, "yeah, we're in favour of the Hindus and Sikhs" will get them out – fine, we'll say that. It costs us nothing and if it gets us a few votes in obscure areas . . . well that's fine.'[16]

In February 2002, matters were made worse when Blunkett attempted to address fears over both British Muslims and asylum-seekers together in a government white paper, 'Secure

Borders, Safe Haven'. This, according to his critics, merely conflated the issues of race and immigration.[17]

The challenge for the BNP was to turn this rising anxiety into seats at the 2002 local elections. In Burnley, Smith extended his DIY publicity techniques, hanging a banner from a thirty-foot mill chimney that overlooked the town's busiest road. BNP cards were left in pubs and at the football ground, directing the public towards a website, Burnleybravepages, which featured rumours about preferential treatment for Asians and asylum-seekers being allowed to jump the queues in doctors' waiting rooms.[18] Smith also began building a database of potential supporters by trawling the telephone directory: 'We knew that our core support was obviously white, for the most part working-class and to a large extent self-employed. Most, if not all, of these could be found in the Yellow Pages under the headings of builders, joiners, electricians, mechanics, etc.'[19]

Backed by an election manifesto that promised regeneration money for 'British' council tenants, plus a crackdown on crime and asylum-seekers, BNP canvassers wheedled their way into voters' minds on the doorstep with the slogan 'Use one vote – make it count!' In 2002, every council seat in Burnley was up for election, with three councillors per ward, so BNP canvassers presented their party as a convenient way to get the attention of mainstream politicians, telling voters to 'give' one out of their three votes to the BNP and the remaining two to mainstream parties, accompanied by the plaintive refrain 'Give us a chance, what do you have to lose?' As one observer of the election count put it:

> The general pattern was for the ballot papers that carried a vote for the BNP – ten thousand of them, over 30 per cent of the ballot papers cast – to be ballot papers carrying two votes for

Labour and one for the BNP. Two votes for the party that – linked to the government – could bring the regeneration funding into the town, and one for the organisation 'fighting for fairer funding', demanding a 'level playing field', so that all Burnley's needy areas could get their 'fair share'.[20]

Richard Chipps was one of many Burnley residents to whom this offer appealed: 'I voted for them because it was a protest that no-one was paying attention to the problems we had. Very few people are actual BNP members. But once you vote for them, people listen.'

By April, the government had become alarmed. Tony Blair gave a front-page interview to the *Lancashire Telegraph* warning people not to vote BNP, while his press secretary Alastair Campbell, a well-known supporter of Burnley football club, came out of a self-imposed media silence to do the same. But it was too late. On 2 May 2002, the repackaged BNP made its first step onto the bottom rung of Britain's political system, winning three council seats.

If voters in Burnley wanted the government's attention, now they had it. Over the weekend of 15 and 16 June, Tony Blair met with senior strategists, chief among them his pollster Philip Gould, who warned that thousands of 'angry young working-class men' were poised to desert Labour for the BNP.[21] There were also danger signs from Europe, where far-right parties were on the rise. In Austria, the slick political operator Joerg Haider had briefly pushed his anti-immigrant Freedom Party into a coalition government in 2000, while in May 2002, Jean-Marie Le Pen of the Front National shocked France's political establishment by reaching the run-off stage against Jacques Chirac in the presidential elections.

France provided a salutary tale: it was the Socialist Party's ratcheting up of anti-immigration rhetoric during the 1980s and 1990s that had paved the way for Le Pen.[22] But Gould, an architect of New Labour, advised triangulation, the strategy which had helped his party defeat the Conservatives by occupying the political space normally held by the right, pushing them further away from the centre. What would it mean to 'occupy' the space held by fascists? After the BNP's shock victory on the Isle of Dogs in 1993, Labour had won back the trust of voters by promising to tackle the housing shortage that had fuelled racist resentment. This time, Gould advised, the party should embrace voters' concerns on immigration and asylum.[23]

In fact, David Blunkett was already doing so. With a reputation for tough pronouncements on law and order, immigration and the need for Muslims to integrate, the home secretary's most notorious moment came during a BBC radio interview a month before the BNP's first victories in Burnley, when he had accused asylum-seekers' children of 'swamping' British schools. I visited Blunkett at his House of Commons office in the autumn of 2011. He denied pandering to racism: 'My use of the word "swamped" was specific. It means "overwhelmed" and if you look at the dictionary definition they're interchangeable,' Blunkett told me, still testy about the incident. Yet while he now regretted his incautious use of wording, he defended the strategy: 'My concern from 2001 onwards was to ensure that we didn't allow that considerable progress that [far-right parties] were making in other parts of Europe to be reflected in Britain.'

Blunkett believed he was in an impossible situation during his time in office, caught 'like a pig in the middle', as he confided to his diary,[24] between his critics on the left and a tabloid press in attack mode. 'We're not racists Mr Blunkett, just terrified for our children's health' read one 2003 headline in the *Sun*, which mounted a campaign accusing asylum-seekers of infecting Britain with HIV, tuberculosis and hepatitis C.[25]

Yet the government's strategy went beyond simply rebutting tabloid criticism; just as Blair, Blunkett and other New Labour grandees made efforts to befriend Rupert Murdoch and the then-editor of the *Sun*, Rebekah Wade (now Brooks), so it actively collaborated in their campaigns. The extent of this collusion was revealed in the summer of 2003 when Downing Street's media planning grid – a calendar on which ministers' publicity engagements were noted in advance – was leaked. For the week of 18 August, the grid entry under 'main news for the week' was '*Sun* asylum week'. On the Monday, the *Sun* was to run a story headlined 'Halt the asylum tide now'; on the Tuesday, 'Our heritage is crumbling'; on the Wednesday, it ran yet another health scare story; and on the Thursday, as noted in advance on Downing Street's grid, was 'Blunkett asylum interview', where the home secretary promised 'draconian' measures to clamp down on bogus claimants.[26]

Beyond this, the government lacked any serious policy to halt the BNP's progress. The riots, followed by the elections in Burnley, had shown that something was wrong in Labour's heartlands, yet Blunkett claims there was a 'lack of collective will' among his cabinet colleagues to do more than triangulate. After the 2003 local elections drew a turnout in England of just 35.6 per cent, Blunkett despaired: 'Tony [Blair] is still not of the mind that real disillusionment has set in . . . It is very hard to get across to someone who believes that everything is fine that the electorate are cheesed off with us.'[27]

A few days after they were elected, Burnley's three new BNP councillors – all local candidates, and none with easily identifiable roots in fascist politics — gave their first press conference. Choosing a patch of wasteland in the deprived ward of Burnley Wood, the image they put forward was that of ordinary Burnley folk, pushed into politics by Labour's neglect of the town. ' "We're just normal people", say BNP trio', ran the headline in the *Burnley Express*.[28] One of the three, David Edwards, told the paper: 'We are just normal people representing the normal people of Burnley. We work and have children.'

The press conference was a propaganda trick: the BNP's breakthrough had not centred on urban Burnley Wood, but on the outlying villages of Cliviger and Worsthorne, which normally voted Tory. This was the only part of the borough that the minuscule local Conservative Party could usually consider a safe bet. Similarly, the areas of Gannow and Rosegrove, where the two other BNP councillors had been elected, were at the smarter end of working-class Burnley.

These relatively well-off voters were the 'builders, joiners, electricians, mechanics, etc.' and were the targets of Smith's leafleting. In many people's minds, support for the far right was a snarl from the most run-down sink estates. But the BNP breakthrough was something else: it was a protest from people who had something to lose, and felt they were in danger of losing it. Resentment appeared to be based on class as well as race. As one BNP voter, a self-employed tradesman who lived in one of the town's more affluent wards, put it: 'It's not that I disapprove of all Pakis, it's all these that's not working, and it's the same with whites. It's not just them, it's whites as well.'[29]

Over the next year, the BNP began to pick up votes away from towns directly affected by the riots — with the asylum panic and worsening attitudes towards Muslims as a backdrop. As the Blair Government beat the drums for war with Iraq, a

BNP councillor was elected in Blackburn after distributing leaflets claiming that the town was to build replicas of the giant arches made of crossed swords installed by Saddam Hussein in Baghdad. The party won a council seat in the Hertfordshire borough of Broxtowe – a white area with no direct experience of immigration – based on a toxic combination of fears about asylum and a deeper-seated hostility to nearby multiracial London.[30] In the 2003 local elections, the BNP won a further six seats on Burnley council, making it the second-largest group – and spread out further into Lancashire and West Yorkshire, winning seats in Halifax. In the latter, as with Burnley, the initial breakthrough came in wards that normally voted Tory.[31]

Yet again, the BNP's own internal tensions hampered progress. While the electoral successes had put an end to the challenge from the Freedom Party, and Eddy Butler had rejoined the BNP, Griffin tried to impose tighter control of the local party in Burnley, scaling down Steven Smith's role.[32] Part of the reason was that Smith made no secret of his support for John Tyndall, who was invited to speak at a Burnley BNP meeting in 2003, against Griffin's instructions. In another instance of fragmentation a year later, Mark Cotterill, a former fundraiser for American Friends of the BNP, who had helped establish links with US-based white supremacist groups, announced he would be standing against the BNP in Blackburn, as a council candidate for the National Front, claiming activists were deserting the BNP because it had 'gone soft'.

In fact, there was compelling evidence to show that the BNP remained a party which nurtured violence and racism. A 2004 BBC documentary, made by an undercover journalist, revealed party activists in Bradford boasting about beating up Asians during the 2001 riots and fantasizing about shooting 'Pakis'. It also featured a secret recording of Griffin addressing a party meeting in Keighley, West Yorkshire, where he expressed his hopes for a riot and described Islam as a 'wicked, vicious faith', claiming that Muslim men were deliberately trying to get white girls pregnant so that they could spread Islam across the world. A young rising star of the BNP, Mark Collett, was also filmed describing asylum-seekers as 'cockroaches'.[33] These comments would lead both to be prosecuted for incitement to racial hatred. They were acquitted in 2006.

The BBC exposé was accompanied by a front-page story in the *Sun*, which bore the headline 'Bloody Nasty People'. If only it were so easy to separate the 'nasty' people from the rest. 'If anyone can tell me who's voting BNP I'd like to know,' pleaded Labour's council leader in Burnley, Stuart Caddy.[34] And while Labour councillors struggled to understand what had happened, the anti-fascist movement too had been thrown into disarray. The Anti-Nazi League tactic of confrontation on the streets worked less well when the BNP was positioning itself as a respectable political party. The group was refused permission to hold an anti-racist concert in Burnley on health and safety grounds, and it drew widespread local criticism when BNP councillors were pelted with eggs and flour as they entered the council chamber for the first time after the 2003 elections.

Julie Waterson, who had been secretary of the Anti-Nazi League since 1992, described it to me as a 'demoralizing' time: 'There was a huge argument on the left about the best way to fight them. [The] Anti-Nazi League was no longer the cutting edge, people were disillusioned with New Labour, which made it hard to get people out on the streets.' In 2003 the Anti-Nazi League was disbanded and a new organization, Unite Against Fascism was established.

In Burnley, Labour's response had been to refuse all co-operation with BNP councillors on official business, while encouraging the perception that the BNP had duped well-meaning but naive Burnley residents into joining them.[35] This appeared to have some effect in 2004, when a sixty-five-year old grandmother, Maureen Stowe, resigned from the BNP to sit as an independent councillor, claiming 'they are not what they seem'.[36]

Others, however, would prove more loyal.

When I phoned Sharon Wilkinson, she was putting her two young grand-daughters to bed. First elected in 2004, fifty-year-old Wilkinson was one of the BNP's few remaining councillors in 2011 – and it was not hard to see why she had retained local support, even as her party's fortunes have receded. Gentle-voiced, Wilkinson explained to me that she joined the BNP because 'as a white person I was being treated differently because of the colour of my skin. By the police, the establishment.' The owner of an off-license, she felt it was unfair that the Asian-run newsagent across the road was given a license to sell alcohol. 'Forty-three people attended the hearing to speak against the license, but they still got it. And that was the whole community that had been ignored. So I stood as a BNP councillor.'

Several Burnley residents I spoke to who opposed the BNP conceded that Wilkinson was good at her job. She certainly seemed to relish the hard, unglamorous slog of local politics, talking enthusiastically to me about her work dealing with dog mess, or successfully winning money for her ward to have traffic calming measures installed.

But when the conversation turned towards the BNP's true

nature, Wilkinson became less confident. Did she think the party was fascist? 'I didn't find that.' Repatriation? 'It's not a reality, is it?' She hesitated, and I could hear a murmuring in the background. 'I'm not against anyone having their own ethnic whatever it is, but let us have ours.'

There was some more murmuring. 'Is that John?' I asked, realizing I had been on speakerphone. 'Hello Daniel,' came a gruff reply. John Cave is a veteran BNP member with 'a stack of membership cards', who believes 'the world needs a leader', preferably in the image of John Tyndall. The BNP handbook states the party should be a 'surrogate family' to its members – but for Cave and Wilkinson this has gone a step further: they got married.

Enoch Powell had been right, Cave told me; in twenty-first-century Britain the immigrant had indeed got the 'whip hand' over the white man. He emphasized that grassroots politics were never anything more than a stepping-stone for the BNP: 'Local politics is boring. And anyone who gets involved in it has to see it from that line of thought that it isn't about doing this and moving a litter bin from A to B or getting the grass cut. In reality the only reason you're there is to give people a chance to say they don't want multiculturalism, they don't want integration and they want, as Mr Tyndall used to say, a white Britain.'

To me, this disturbing encounter illustrated just why the BNP seemed to have outfoxed their opponents in the early 2000s. As Steven Smith recalled, the cry of 'Nazis' did not seem to match what many people saw for themselves. A few days before the local elections in 2003, he explained, anti-fascists distributed a leaflet that bore a picture of Burnley town hall superimposed with a giant swastika and the slogan 'Is this what you really want?'

'Now then,' Smith said. 'Bearing in mind that not many days after that leaflet was circulated, the Burnley electorate voted for another six BNP councillors, there's one of two things you can say: Either people weren't put off by it – or perhaps they weren't too averse to it. I'll leave you to draw your own conclusions.'

7

We're the Labour Party Your Parents Voted for

Sitting between the fruit machine and the bar at the British Legion club on Dagenham's Becontree estate, Darryl was explaining to me why he thought his neighbourhood had gone downhill. 'It used to be nice and clean round here. Go down my road now and some dirty sod's chucked out an old mattress.' As we spoke, children were running between crowded tables, clutching glasses of orange squash and dodging the Legion's staff as they doled out tickets for the Wednesday evening raffle. Often, before the raffle, the names of British soldiers killed in action are read out, and black ribbons pinned to the Legion's standard. 'We're lucky tonight,' the club's secretary had told me. 'There haven't been any this week.'

The Legion has been a centre of social life on Becontree for almost eighty years, and it shows no signs of diminishing, at least not when I visited. Yet to twenty-nine-year-old Darryl, who has lived his whole life here, Becontree 'doesn't feel like home any more'. What had changed, then? 'Well . . .' he gave a hesitant roll of the eyes. 'It's full of Africans, innit?' His voice quickened: 'they're all coming here from Westminster. My dad sold his house and an African family took it. They got fifty grand to move. Why can't I get fifty grand to move? If they get fifty grand to move over here, why can't I get fifty grand to move away from them?'

When we met, Darryl was enjoying a quiet drink before he set off for his night shift as a track engineer on the London Underground. He explained to me that he was a proud member of the RMT, the militant transport workers' union renowned for its ability to stick up for its members' interests. 'Look what Bob Crow[1] got us – a 5 per cent pay package, while everyone else is getting one per cent, two per cent or nothing.' We were speaking in June 2011, the day before 750,000 public sector workers were to go on strike in defence of their pensions, and Darryl was firmly behind them. 'They want me to work until I'm seventy. Why pay my taxes and work til I'm dead? I don't like the Conservatives, I don't like what they're doing to the NHS.'

You might reasonably have assumed that Darryl was a Labour man; a working-class, unionized voter in a constituency[2] that had consistently returned a Labour MP since 1945. But he had been voting BNP for the best part of a decade. Why? Weren't Labour the party of the working class? 'Yeah, but they give it to the wrong people,' he retorted, singling out asylum-seekers. 'I go to Morrisons and I'm paying for my food with the money I've earned and someone who can't speak English is there and they're paying with vouchers they've been given. I think the government should look after their own people before they look after the immigrants. They should look after people who fought in the war.'

This, Darryl insisted, made neither him nor the BNP racist. 'White people aren't better than everyone else, I wouldn't say that, not in any way. Ninety per cent of doctors are Asian and you can't get better doctors than them.' He continued: 'I do a lot for the poppy – I was at Tesco in Goodmayes [near Dagenham] and there's a lot of Asians around there. I wasn't expecting to get much out of them but I was shocked at the amount of Indians who put in the pot. They had a lot of respect. Cos they all fought in the war. The black Jamaicans, most of them do work, pay their taxes. But it's the people who come over here and ponce off the state. I'm a working man, I pay my taxes, they get more than I'm entitled to. It's not fair.'

It was through this pervasive sense of 'unfairness' that the British National Party insinuated itself into the minds of residents on Dagenham's Becontree estate. By the end of 2006, the party had twelve members elected to Barking and Dagenham council, the tip of a wave of successes that saw upwards of forty councillors elected in towns across England's North and Midlands, and on the outer fringes of London. The next three years, leading up to 2009, were as close as Nick Griffin ever got to seeing his 'ladder strategy' – climbing the rungs of government from the bottom upwards – bear fruit. As it was, even these relatively minor successes were enough to hasten the entry of a new character onto the political stage: the white working class; 'Britain's lost tribe' according to one newspaper. But who were they? And what did being white have to do with it?

By 2005, there was one thing upon which Nick Griffin and the political establishment could appear to agree: democracy was in crisis. That year, an official commission, prompted by a record low turnout at the 2001 general election, surveyed thousands of members of the public and concluded that there was a 'well-ingrained popular view across the country that our political institutions and their politicians are failing, untrustworthy, and disconnected from the great mass of the British people.'[3]

This wasn't the government's problem alone: turnout at general elections had been falling steadily since 1992 and party membership showed an even longer-term decline, with both Labour and Conservative membership around a tenth of its peak in the 1950s. As the conservative political journalist Peter Oborne has argued, this mass disconnect from politics was partly a reaction to an increasingly insular Westminster, where MPs formed a 'comfortable club' with think tanks, lobbyists and the media.[4] This political bubble left the majority of the population excluded, but it was primarily working-class voters who were abandoning the polls. It was they who comprised the majority of the five million voters who deserted Labour between 1997 and 2010, while the Tories, who once attracted nearly half of working-class voters, had never recovered the support that they lost after Thatcher.[5]

Griffin attempted to tap into this mood with a manifesto for the 2005 general election that attempted to convince the public that the BNP was 'neither a single-issue party nor an ephemeral protest group'. Titled 'Rebuilding British Democracy', it declared that 'As British voters, we are repeatedly told that we live in an elective democracy; whereas in truth what exists is a sham and an illusion. Genuine democracy, where the population's will is given expression by the elected representatives, is starkly absent from Britain.'[6]

Over fifty-four pages, the manifesto sets out what Griffin called a 'major ideological revamp'. In fact it was a reworking of familiar themes, reflecting his own personal trajectory in far-right politics. Reflecting the anti-authoritarian strain of thought that Griffin had explored in his youth, the manifesto praised the Magna Carta, advocating a new Bill of Rights and Swiss-style 'citizens' initiative referenda'. It attacked the current system of devolution as putting power in the hands of 'a faceless and relatively remote bureaucracy' and called instead for the establishment of an English parliament and the further devolution of power to county councils. The BNP had been winning the majority of its seats in England and the idea of a suppressed English identity was given further emphasis by a decision to launch the manifesto on St George's Day. On foreign policy, troops were to be withdrawn immediately from Afghanistan and Iraq, and used instead to defend Britain's borders.

Mimicking the worker-oriented policies of the National Front Strasserites ('We are not Marxists – We are not Capitalists', as their slogan went), the manifesto praised 'strong unions and strong industries', called for a 'free, fully-funded National Health Service for all British citizens' and bemoaned the loss of a million manufacturing jobs under New Labour. It proposed that workers take part-ownership of industry, and that an interventionist, 'Britain First' economic policy be adopted as a counter to the dictates of a 'corrupt, unaccountable' European Union and 'the reigning myth of economics . . . that there is very little a government can do about its economy other than submit to the dictates of the international marketplace.'

Although the emphasis had shifted, racism was still at the core of the BNP's programme and the manifesto devoted considerable space to attacking immigration, which 'threatened . . . Britain's very existence'. Instead, the party promised an end to 'positive discrimination' and claimed that 'multiculturalism' was 'a profound cultural war against the British people', waged by an elite who sought 'to create a new ethnic power base to replace the working class which they have abandoned in pursuit of their enthusiasm for globalisation, justified by a quasi-Marxist ideology of the equality of all cultures.'

Echoing the 'clash of civilizations' view of Islam, which had grown in currency among western intellectuals since 2001, the manifesto opposed the proposed expansion of the EU into Bulgaria, Romania, and subsequently Turkey. This would bring seventy-five million Muslims into Europe and 'mark the end of Europe's ancient and historic close identification with Christendom, and the beginning of the end of secular democratic government in the West'. Anti-Islam sentiment was of growing importance to the BNP, since it had mainstream support, but the manifesto also showed a trace of anti-Semitism in attacking media owned by 'foreigners whose primary loyalty is not to Britain'. It also proposed arming the population and introducing a new criminal offence to prevent 'the deliberate dissemination of falsehoods' by any media outlet. Beneath the democratic sheen, all the building blocks of fascism remained: the evocation of a mortal threat to the nation; the hint of conspiracy theory; the nod towards violence and repression.[7]

BNP activists were issued with a new set of guidelines to reinforce the shift in presentation. According to the Orwellian-sounding 'Language and Concepts and Discipline Manual' published in 2005, the BNP was never to be referred to as 'fascist', but as a 'right-wing populist party . . . we espouse, like many political parties all over the world, the right-of-centre views traditional to ordinary working people who are not leftists'.

The strengthened appeal to working-class voters[8] was, in fact, an indication of failure. The BNP had again lost out to UKIP in the 2004 European elections and the dream of a far-right movement that could unite 'the neglected and oppressed white working class' with 'the frustrated and disorientated traditional middle class', as Griffin had set his sights on at the start of his leadership, seemed unattainable for the moment. But the 'revamp' seemed to be working. At the 2005 election, the party received nearly 200,000 votes, four times the number it had in 2001, doing well in Yorkshire, the North East and outer London. A year later, as the party prepared to stand a record four hundred candidates in local elections, an opinion poll suggested that a majority of respondents agreed with BNP policies when they were not told which party they belonged to.[9]

This was less of a surprise than it might sound, as the BNP's declared policies were intended to make the party seem moderate, and the 2005 election was dominated by the issue of immigration, thanks to the Conservative tactic of 'dog-whistle' politics, imported from Australia via the strategist Lynton Crosby. Under Michael Howard, the Tories campaigned under the suggestive slogan 'are you thinking what we're thinking?' and posters that read 'it's not racist to impose limits on immigration'. Surely, though, it would take more than word games for the BNP to actually win elections?

Darren Rodwell remembers vividly the day that BNP activists turned up in his local park on the Becontree estate. 'They were in our local park, giving out literature, giving discs with music on.' As the head of a tenant's association, and with a combative sense of local pride to boot, Rodwell spoke out. 'I challenged them. I said you don't represent us, go away.' Then he did what anyone would do when they're visited by unwanted pests: phoned the council.

By the time officers from Barking and Dagenham council had organized a response, many months later, the BNP had already sunk its roots into the community. The reason they were in the park was to carry out a favourite propaganda exercise, the 'clean-up' team. Dressed in high-vis jackets, emblazoned with the party logo, BNP activists were picking up litter, introducing themselves to the parents who brought their children to the park, and offering to clean up any unwanted rubbish from the surrounding streets. The next step would be to photograph themselves at work, print the photos on leaflets and distribute them to houses nearby. As the BNP activist hand-book advised: 'Never forget a picture is worth a thousand words. Most voters aren't interested in our political views, but they will respond positively to anything they can see us doing to make their area and their lives a little better.'[10] This was 'community politics', BNP style: practical campaign techniques borrowed from the Liberal Democrats, backed up by Nick Griffin's theories about 'counter-power' and establishing 'cultural hegemony' at the grass roots.

Yet litter is hardly unique to Barking and Dagenham. So why, then, would a neighbourhood clean-up campaign have such purchase on an estate like Becontree? Part of the answer lies in the place itself. To call Becontree an 'estate' underplays its scale: It is a vast, planned community built in the 1920s to house 27,000 families moved from the slums of London's East End and still the largest public housing development in the world. It sits on the outer fringes of the capital, occupying most of the borough of Barking and Dagenham, where urban London blends into suburban Essex sprawl. Nor does it fit the stereo-type of tower blocks and concrete walkways; Becontree's neat brick semis, with front and back gardens are arranged on long, tree-lined avenues and quiet cul-de-sacs.

But the homes, owned and rented out by the council, were tightly regulated. It was intended to be a model town with a socially improving mission – to teach the unruly working classes the values of 'respectable' middle-class life and tenants had to abide by strict rules regarding the upkeep of their properties. One of the benefits of this set-up was that residents could maintain the strong ties of kinship they had established in the East End. People here tended to have their children young and families are close. Indeed, as one of the borough's two MPs, Margaret Hodge, told me, 'it has not been uncommon to find three generations of one family living within a short walk of one another.'

At forty-one, with one grown-up child, and several younger ones, Rodwell was in many ways typical of Dagenham's longer-term residents. He was born here, went to school here and most of his family lived nearby. But in one important respect, he differed. 'Many moons ago,' he says, 'my father said to me: don't ever work in Ford's.'

'Ford's', as the once-imposing automobile plant that borders the neighbourhood is referred to locally, was another defining factor in Barking and Dagenham's history. In the 1920s, Becontree's population, decanted from the bustling city to a somewhat isolated periphery, was an attractive prospect for the corporation, which preferred to locate its global network of factories in remote areas with captive, cheap-to-employ populations. The American car manufacturer established a plant in 1931, which grew to employ 40,000 people at its peak in the 1980s.

Ford defined Dagenham. It didn't just provide jobs; it sustained a network of pubs, social clubs, a football team and even a brass band that could hold its own against more famous rivals. 'We were like a mining town in the North,' says Rodwell, 'only just on the edge of London.'

A thriving industry was met by thriving trade unionism,

which gave Dagenham its third great constant: the Labour Party. In local elections Labour candidates stood almost unopposed until the BNP arrived, and it was not uncommon for all fifty-odd seats on the council to be occupied by Labour. 'This was an area where you could put a monkey up, stick a Labour rosette on it and it would have got elected,' more than one Dagenham resident quipped to me.

One-party rule of this sort is not a healthy political culture – but tolerable, so long as the jobs and the homes are plentiful. But from the 1980s onwards a series of shocks destroyed such certainties. The first was the Right to Buy scheme. The Thatcher Government's sell-off of council housing was attractive to many Dagenham residents, who took advantage of it and bought their own homes. As a result, the number of houses on the council's books declined rapidly. Thatcher's object may have been to 'change the soul', converting the working classes into property owners, but paradoxically, Dagenham remained proud of its identity – and many residents still expected the council to provide for them.

The second shock was the slow loss of jobs at Ford's. With a global network of factories, the company was – and still is – able to switch production of its cars to wherever labour costs and currency exchange rates give the most favourable returns. During the 1990s, Dagenham became less and less attractive to Ford's accountants. A plant still operates there, but it employs 4,000 people, a tenth of what it once did. And while capital was deserting Dagenham, its arrival in the heart of London was creating a new pressure. The rise of a world financial centre, focused on Canary Wharf, drove up inner London property prices and made Dagenham a newly attractive prospect for buyers.

As Rodwell explained to me, 'we always expected Ford to be there. Once Ford decided that was it, it was a massive economic and social disaster for the borough. People who under dear old Margaret Thatcher got the right to buy their house with a 70 per cent discount or similar did so while they were earning good money at Ford's, and when Ford said enough's enough, those people were sitting on a phenomenal asset, because they'd had such a good discount, half the housing stock had been sold – 19,000 out of the 40,000 odd council houses.'

What happens when an older generation all decide to sell up at roughly the same time? In a period of just a few years, says Rodwell, the population changed dramatically. 'It started in 2002, but by 2004 or 2005 you could see a really stark change in the borough. Something like one in five families moved out in a six-year period, so that's 20 per cent of your community gone.'

In a short space of time, Barking and Dagenham changed from a settled, mainly white community to an ethnic mix that began to resemble the rest of London. Many of the ex-council homes were sold on to private landlords, who split them up into flats and crammed in as many tenants as they could. Further pressure came from inner London councils, who would cope with their own housing shortage by placing tenants in private accommodation in Barking and Dagenham, where rents were cheaper. More tenants meant more mess – and suddenly the neighbourhood didn't look like it used to.

School records (the most accurate information until the 2011 census is published) indicate that Barking and Dagenham had a lower rate of population change than most other London boroughs.[11] But it had still taken place rapidly and, according to Rodwell, the Labour Party simply was not there to explain. Because council and parliamentary candidates felt so safe, they barely even bothered to canvass: for years, there was no direct contact between thousands of residents and their political representatives. Instead, people put two and two together, blaming the borough's chronic shortage of council housing on the new arrivals. As one resident told a focus group in 2006:

> I work for the youngsters and they can't afford properties. They really can't. If you think, the cheapest property is £130,000 that I know of. They can't afford to buy and they go to [the] council and they say 'We're not entertaining'. It's annoying. Then you think you've got the asylum-seekers, they're giving them properties and they don't look after them and your own can't get on the property ladder.[12]

For the BNP, the clean-up campaign was just the first step. The party members then distributed a newsletter titled *Dagenham Patriot* that claimed that Labour-run councils in East London were operating a secret 'Africans for Essex' scheme whereby immigrant families from inner London were being given grants of £5,000 to buy houses in Dagenham. The propaganda linked this to a wider disenchantment, stating: 'The Labour Party treat you with contempt: it's time you treated them the same way!'[13]

'Africans' was a catch-all term that referred to second or third generation black Londoners who'd moved out from inner London, as well as new arrivals – but it worked. In 2004, the BNP won a council by-election in Goresbrook ward on Becontree, using a tactic they called 'stealth campaigning'.[14] First, activists drafted in from across London and the South East canvassed every house in the ward, determining who might consider voting for the BNP. They then repeatedly canvassed and leafleted those homes, avoiding any house with known Labour voters or black inhabitants, so that opponents would not notice their efforts. Although the campaign focused on housing, it was still founded on racism: as the BNP's group development officer Tony Lecomber told an undercover reporter, 'At the end of the day, it's a racial thing. We're the BNP, we are who we are because of race. We don't want blacks here.' (For this slip, the veteran BNP activist was removed from his position by Griffin.)

The next step was to infiltrate the local tenants' and residents' associations (TRAs). As Lawrence Rustem, a BNP activist who would subsequently be elected to Barking and Dagenham council, explained, the idea was to 'act as a councillor even though you may not yet be one'. BNP members were advised to attend their TRA meetings, where 'you will find out what the problems are within your local community . . . your face will become known.' Once a 'problem', such as an untidy front garden, or an unkempt hedge, had been solved, activists were told to 'slip into the discussions that you're the local BNP and that it has been the local British National Party who have sorted things out.'[15]

At the 2005 general election, the BNP received its best result – 16.9 per cent of the vote – in Barking, a constituency that covers the majority of Becontree. The real prize, however, were the 2006 local elections. Shortly before voters went to the polls that year, alarm was raised by Barking's Labour MP Margaret Hodge, who told the *Sunday Telegraph* that canvass returns suggested most of her constituents were considering voting BNP.

Hodge, more than anyone, should have known the difference that council housing made to people's lives. In a previous political incarnation, as a fiercely left-wing leader of Islington council during the 1970s and 1980s, she had made sure that new council homes were built in order to stop the borough's working-class population being pushed out by gentrification. But as a minister at the heart of the New Labour establishment, Hodge was not willing to admit that a key element of the modernizing project appeared to have failed – in 2006, with Blair having delivered a historic third term, such honesty was not an option. People couldn't get council houses because thousands had been sold off and none built to replace them. Yet Hodge skated over this uncomfortable truth, implicitly endorsing the BNP's racism instead. Voters in Barking were angry 'because they can't get a home for their children,' Hodge told her interviewer. 'They see black and ethnic minority communities moving in and they are angry.'

When eleven BNP councillors were elected to Barking and Dagenham council in 2006, Hodge was widely condemned and the GMB trade union called for her to resign. In reality, her intervention, a couple of days before the election, had come far too late to have any real effect on the result, but it emphasized a much deeper problem. Across England, the BNP had doubled its number of council seats, from twenty-two to forty-four; the majority in previously solid Labour towns.

'I'm not pleased about it,' said Peter Hain, with just a hint of told-you-so in his voice, 'but my warnings were prophetic'. Hain, a former New Labour minister and founding member of the Anti-Nazi League, was telling me about an interview he gave to the *New Statesman* in 1999, where he warned that his party's relentless focus on Middle England risked being 'gratuitously offensive' to its working-class supporters. Across thirteen years in government, this strategy took its toll: 'Labour,' said Hain, 'ceased to be seen as the party that spoke for the interests of working-class people. There was a failure to deliver on housing, there was grotesque wealth at the top, it was a tough time for anyone facing job insecurity.'

While New Labour's chief ideologues promoted the idea that class divisions were no longer relevant – part of the 'old ways of working and doing things', in Tony Blair's words – working-class people of all races were feeling the sharp end of the New Labour project. Inequality of income, which had soared under Margaret Thatcher, continued to rise.[16] In 2004, well before the financial crash, real wages stagnated for the bottom half of earners and fell for the bottom third.[17] Disguised by the availability of cheap credit, social mobility had in fact stalled. The aspirations of many were increasingly out of reach.

Plentiful immigration, which grew further after 2004, when eight former Eastern Bloc countries joined the EU, was only one factor in keeping wages low – a 'flexible' labour market, where employers were much freer to hire and fire than elsewhere in Europe, was the broader picture – but fears about immigration were hyped by right-wing newspapers and pressure groups such as Migration Watch. Perception mattered: by the end of the New Labour era, only 18 per cent saw immigration as a problem in their area, but 76 per cent saw it as a national problem.[18]

In 2009, Gordon Brown's attempt to deal with growing discontent as the economy turned sour was a disastrous speech in which he promised 'British jobs for British workers' – a slogan that could have come straight out of a far-right propaganda handbook, and one that was thrown back in his face in 2009 by oil refinery workers in Lincolnshire, who staged wildcat strikes in protest at their wages and conditions being undercut by several hundred European contract workers. Even this ham-fisted attempt to address the issue was too late. During New Labour's pomp, Hain told me, few at the top were willing to listen. Blair, along with his closest allies, simply did not see a problem. According to Hain, his warning in 1999 was met with a complacent response. 'Peter Mandelson said to me, "your preoccupation with the working-class vote is wrong. They've got nowhere to go."'

Or did they? In Barking and Dagenham, the BNP threw its efforts into giving these voters a new home, with the doorstep promise: 'We're the Labour Party your parents voted for.' Griffin's ambition was for local councillors to take symbolic stands against government policy, drawing his inspiration from the actions of early Labour councils, such as the Poplar rates strike of 1921. The idea was that through this posturing, the BNP would fashion a 'reputational shield' – that is, the party would gain a reputation for more than simply being anti-immigration.[19]

Progress towards this goal was limited. The announcement of the annual budget is the most important date on the local government calendar, and opposition councillors are given the opportunity to put forward alternative proposals, outlining how they would have spent the year's money. Yet in 2007, BNP councillors in Barking and Dagenham failed even to submit proposals – a surprise, given that the group leader, Richard Barnbrook, was in charge of national training sessions for BNP councillors – and instead put out leaflets claiming that they had been prevented from asking questions.[20]

Indeed, Barnbrook provided a good example of how the BNP project was limited by the calibre of its activists. A trained artist who was regarded as charismatic in relation to his party colleagues, Barnbrook had been tipped as a future leader – one who could more successfully promote the BNP's image as a moderate, 'right-wing populist' party. When he was elected to the London Assembly in 2008 (in addition to his position on Barking and Dagenham council), he seemed an articulate advocate of the BNP's propaganda, promising to work for Londoners regardless of 'colour or identity' yet criticizing 'multiculturalism', which he claimed meant 'a small minority get a large proportion of the finance paid by . . . the majority that fund this city.'

Yet Barnbrook made little impact and was censured for bringing his office into disrepute after he made false claims in a video interview, posted on his website in September 2008, that there had been a string of knife murders in Barking and Dagenham. The same year, Labour councillors were able to score an easy victory against the BNP, when they put forward a motion congratulating Britain's Olympic athletes – a typically multiracial squad – for their successes in Beijing. BNP councillors voted against, their racism apparently taking precedence over their patriotism.

Slowly, the party learned how to position itself more convincingly. Alternative budget proposals in subsequent years made gestures to 'old Labour' policies: the party offered, for example, to buy back £4 million worth of homes for council housing; to set up credit union facilities at the council's One Stop Shops; and to cut charges for Meals on Wheels. (These were to be funded by cuts that included closing down the council's equality and diversity team).[21]

Publicity material emphasized a range of popular grievances with New Labour: the borough's two MPs, Margaret Hodge and Jon Cruddas were criticized for their alleged personal wealth (Hodge is the daughter of a millionaire steel trader;

Cruddas owns two homes) and for having supported the Iraq War. It also carried a story about a French construction firm, which had won contracts under the Private Finance Initiative to build two schools in the borough, pointing out the company's 'truly shocking record for laying off British workers and importing cheap foreign labour to drive down wages.'[22]

Nationally, how many of the BNP's voters really were disgruntled Labour supporters? It's true that a significant proportion of BNP supporters held 'working-class' occupations. According to one typical poll, conducted shortly before the 2009 European elections, 69 per cent of BNP voters came from the social classifications C2 (skilled manual workers) and DE (those with semi-skilled or unskilled manual jobs).[23] Among these, the BNP was particularly likely to attract the skilled working classes, and was most successful in areas with large concentrations of employed skilled workers. Yet BNP voters appeared only marginally more likely to come from Labour-voting families – 47 per cent, compared to an overall figure of 43 per cent. A quarter came from Conservative backgrounds, and the rest from elsewhere.[24]

Unsurprisingly, perhaps, BNP voters named immigration as the greatest problem facing the country: 60 per cent of BNP voters surveyed between 2002 and 2006 said immigration was the greatest problem facing the country, compared to 16 per cent overall,[25] while in 2009, 95 per cent of BNP voters surveyed said they wanted a total halt to immigration.[26] And in 2009, more than half of BNP voters read newspapers that were hostile to immigration (*Daily Mail*, *Daily Express* and *Daily Star*). Yet for the majority of these voters, their objections were cultural rather than economic: 81 per cent, for instance, agreed with the proposition that Islam was 'a danger to Western civilisation'. A substantial minority also held deeply racist views: 45 per cent agreed that non-whites were 'not really British'; 31 per cent agreed that black people were 'intellectually inferior'; and 33 per cent agreed that there was a 'conspiracy by Jews and Communists to undermine the West'.[27]

What this showed was that the BNP had failed to spread very far beyond a racist core of support. In Barking and Dagenham, Burnley, and other ex-industrial towns where the BNP found success, the party was only able to progress because of a much wider working-class disengagement from politics. The number of voters who chose the BNP was far smaller, for instance, than the number of Labour voters who simply abstained. Yet when the political and media elite began to wake up to this disengagement, it was on the terms of race, rather than class – a distortion that suited the BNP's agenda.

At the beginning of 2008 the BBC, partly in response to the rise of the BNP, broadcast its White Season, a major new series of programmes that asked 'Is white working-class Britain becoming invisible?' The short answer should have been yes, but not because of race: working-class representation in politics and the media had plummeted in recent decades.[28] Instead, the series, which was timed to coincide with the fortieth anniversary of Enoch Powell's 'rivers of blood' speech and featured a sympathetic reappraisal of the politician, sought to portray white working-class people as an endangered ethnic group. One trailer for the series showed a white male face being written on in foreign languages by non-white hands, until his face was obscured. As the commissioning editor, Richard Klein, explained in a piece for the *Daily Mail*, BBC opinion polls suggested that 'many of the white working class see themselves as an oppressed ethnic minority . . . in part of the consequence of multiculturalism': 'They complain of double standards and hypocrisy, pointing out that the media revel in telling stories of Asian and African immigrants, but ignores tales from the white working class. Every other culture, they argue, is revered except that of the indigenous population.'[29]

The research actually indicated that 'the most powerful' working-class grievance was in fact with New Labour – an explicitly political complaint – but the BBC made a deliberate decision to focus on race and culture instead. In this, the broadcaster was merely following the tide. The right-wing backlash against 'multiculturalism' that had flared up in 1999 after the Macpherson report, and again after the riots of 2001, had by now been endorsed by significant sections of liberal opinion. In 2004, Trevor Phillips, the head of the Commission for Racial Equality, announced that multiculturalism should be 'killed off', singling out 'young Muslims', who 'should work by the rules of British people'. A year later, after the 7/7 bombings, Phillips gave a speech where he warned that Britain was 'sleepwalking into segregation'.

The idea that the real divisions in twenty-first-century Britain centred on race and culture, rather than wealth, was an interpretation of events that conveniently suited the BNP's own aims. Yet its image as a party that defended the white working-class in particular was a deliberately crafted propaganda trick, which relied on concealing elements of its own doctrine. As its own Language and Concepts Discipline Manual stated: '. . . arguments for our policies should always be couched in language calculated to be relevant to the interests of that audience. Do not bore a workingmen's audience with those parts of our ideology that derive from old-school Toryism, or puzzle an affluent suburban audience with an explanation of worker ownership of industry.'

In 2006, an undercover investigation of the BNP's central London branch by the *Guardian* discovered that members included company directors, computing entrepreneurs, bankers and estate agents. One was a servant of the Queen who lived at Buckingham Palace, while another, Simone Clarke, was principal dancer with the English National Ballet.[30] Two years later, the national membership list was leaked online, revealing that the BNP had grown significantly since Griffin assumed leadership, from under 3,000 members to well over 10,000. Analysis of the list indicated that while a significant proportion of members came from skilled working-class occupations, senior roles were given to activists with a long history of involvement in fascist politics.[31] As an editorial in *Identity* warned in early 2009, there was a danger in being perceived as a 'class party': 'Since its foundation the BNP has transcended the divisions of class. We have as many members today who have in the past voted Conservative as those who have voted Labour . . . the key thing about those in the white working class who now support us is that they do WORK . . . they look down with contempt upon the benefit scroungers who have never worked and do not intend to.'

Even as the BNP appeared to be an emerging new force in local politics, many white working-class people were brave enough to voice their disgust in public. The West Yorkshire town of Keighley was briefly home to the BNP's strongest council seat in the country, where it benefited from what might be described as a perfect storm of local and national circumstances. Like

Burnley, the town had a long history of economic neglect, and a perception among some residents that regeneration money was being unfairly spent on 'Asian' areas.[32]

But there was a further twist. In 2004, Channel 4 broadcast a documentary about the sex grooming of teenage girls by gangs of adult men. Angela Sinfield, a Keighley resident whose twelve-year-old daughter had been repeatedly abused by several adult men over the course of a year, had collaborated anonymously with the programme makers. She had found it impossible to get police to intervene, since the law at the time did not permit 'hearsay' evidence: if her daughter were being abused she would have to make a complaint herself. With the help of her local MP, Ann Cryer, Sinfield was campaigning for a change in the law to permit hearsay evidence and to make grooming a criminal offence.

The attraction for the BNP was that most, although not all, cases of suspected grooming under police review involved Asian men. It claimed credit for the Channel 4 programme and that it alone had 'exposed' the issue of grooming, since the issue drew together some of the party's favourite propaganda themes: white resentment at Asians and a fear of Muslim culture. It was in Keighley in 2004 that Griffin made his speech describing Islam as a 'wicked, vicious faith'. In 2005 he stood for parliament there, and now through the Sinfield case, the BNP could project an image of threatened white motherhood.

According to fascist lore, it was just this threat to women that would spark a revival of the white race. An article published in *Identity* magazine entitled 'The awakening of dormant femininity', laid out this philosophy, stating 'the only thing which can destroy a folk group is forced integration, and as this threat of extinction is now upon us, it will not be long before the powerful maternal instincts of womanhood awaken.'[33] What made the grooming issue so useful was that it provided a way for the BNP to link its own Nazi-derived biological racism – shared only by a tiny fraction of the voting public – with the much broader climate of fear over Islam, and the growing narrative that white working-class people had been wronged by multiculturalism. 'There is a problem with these people, with creeping Islamification of Britain,' a BNP spokesman told the *Guardian*. 'No one else will talk about these things and people who live in a democracy should have the right to have their concerns aired.'[34]

In 2004, the BNP won a council seat in Keighley with 51 per cent of the vote after distributing a leaflet with quotes from Sinfield purporting to endorse the BNP and its 'campaign group', Mothers Against Paedophilia. This so incensed Sinfield that she decided to speak out. 'I have never met with Mr Griffin. I have never had anything to do with the BNP . . . they are just a bunch of racists,' she told the anti-fascist magazine *Searchlight*. 'The BNP have never spoken to me and do not know me, so when they take what has actually happened to me and twist it and turn it to favour them, I think it is disgusting.'[35]

Backed by a coalition of anti-fascist groups, trade union branches and the local Labour Party, Sinfield headed a campaign against the BNP. The strategy was to confront the grooming issue head on – but as an issue of crime, rather than of race or culture. As Sinfield said, 'The truth is that a lot of these men are Asian men but I am not racist. It is about criminality.'

In 2006, she stood against the BNP in the local elections – a decision that required no small amount of personal courage, given that at one point her own brother was proposed as the BNP candidate. Sinfield, standing as a Labour candidate, narrowly beat her BNP rival. Here was a white working-class woman who refused to accept the role the BNP wanted her to play; and who refused to accept the pessimism about a multiracial society that radiated from sections of the establishment. As she told the *Guardian*, 'I've never thought of myself as a politician, but why not stand up to these people? I'm a local woman, I know a lot of people and I know what damage the BNP are doing round here.' In a further twist, Sinfield's campaign had been organized through mothers who used Keighley's Sure Start childcare centre – Sure Start being a rare New Labour project that all could agree had improved the lives of working-class people.[36]

The BNP may have played on people's despondency, but their views were never in the majority. Sinfield's victory was a sign of what could happen if their opponents had the courage and support to speak out.

8

Good Fences Make Good Neighbours

It was a humid July day in Strasbourg, and inside the Louise Weiss building, it felt like the start of school term. Journalists and politicians, assembled for the 2009 opening of the European Parliament, were greeting each other like old friends outside the main debating chamber, known in a typical piece of EU jargon as the hemicycle. Here, in the glass and pine atrium of this imposing cylindrical edifice – Britain's contribution to which is a garish floral carpet in the staff bar that bears more than a hint of cross-Channel ferry – you could spot the celebrities of European politics, such as Daniel Cohn-Bendit, the revolutionary student leader-turned-Green, strolling around, pursued by an entourage of admirers.

Hidden away, however, at the end of a winding corridor in a far-flung administrative block, a more furtive gathering was taking place. Convened by a member of Austria's anti-immigrant Freedom Party, it was a meeting of the *non-inscrits*, 'non-attached' MEPs who had not been invited to join any of the main coalitions in parliament. Aside from a few mavericks, such as a member of Northern Ireland's Democratic Unionist Party, this meant the far right.

Wanting to get a bit closer, I removed my bright yellow press badge, slipped it into my pocket and loitered by the conference room door as people filed in: members of Jobbik, a Hungarian fascist movement that boasts its own uniformed militia; Jean-Marie Le Pen and his daughter Marine, who at that point was being groomed to take over leadership of the Front National; assorted members of Belgium's Flemish Interest and others. Then, ambling down the corridor, came two of the newest additions to the parliament: Nick Griffin and Andrew Brons, accompanied by Griffin's wife, and a minder in an ill-fitting suit.

In June 2009, British voters sent the leader of the BNP, along with the sixty-one-year-old Brons, who began his political career in Colin Jordan's National Socialist Movement, to the European Parliament. With over sixty councillors, a London Assembly member and, now, two MEPs, this was the BNP's peak, in a year where public satisfaction with mainstream politics reached its nadir. Britain was in recession, Gordon Brown's prime ministership was foundering, and in the spring of 2009, the Westminster expenses scandal crystallized the perception that the country was being run by a self-serving elite.

The BNP aimed its £500,000 election campaign squarely at this discontent, with a slogan 'Punish the Pigs' and a manifesto that advocated an immediate halt to immigration and withdrawal from the EU to fix the country's economic woes. The glossy booklet it came in was derided by opponents for its use of cheap stock photography – in particular, a World War Two Spitfire that on closer inspection turned out to have come from a Polish air force squadron – but the manifesto concluded with a familiar refrain: 'British Jobs for British Workers'.

The BNP was not the only political outsider offering anti-EU, anti-immigrant populism. 'Now is the moment to register a protest vote,' advised the *Daily Express* in a leader on 3 June, although it warned its readers against voting BNP, reminding them that 'Britain is known throughout the world as the country that spearheaded the defeat of fascism in Europe.' But while fascist politics were beyond the pale for the *Express*, anti-immigrant politics were not. The *Express* recommended a vote for UKIP, whose leader Nigel Farage praised Enoch Powell shortly before the elections as 'an extraordinary fellow. I admired him for having the guts to talk about an issue that seemed to be really rather important: immigration, society, how do we want to live in this country.'

When the results came in, the right was in no doubt about the significance of the BNP's two victories. According to one *Telegraph* columnist, it sent the message that 'many decent people, who are not xenophobic but feel under siege by alien cultures, want an end to mass immigration before the melting pot boils over.' White Britons were 'never consulted' about immigration; 'this is the democratic deficit that the BNP exploits.'[1] The *Express* agreed: 'Labour's belief in multiculturalism has led to the establishment of ghettos populated by non-integrated ethnic groups from the Third World,' wrote the paper's political editor on 9 June. 'Many of the areas that saw a rise in the BNP vote have also borne the brunt of excessive immigration.'

Yet just as in 2004, UKIP were the real beneficiaries of a right-wing backlash: the party won almost two and a half million votes, coming second overall – ahead of Labour and the Lib Dems. What's more, discontent with mainstream politics swung to the left as well: the Green Party received 1.2 million votes and gained two seats in London and the South East.

In comparison, the BNP had not much improved on their total, attracting just 140,000 extra votes. However Labour's vote – and the overall turnout – had dropped so much that

Griffin and Brons crossed the threshold demanded by the system of proportional representation and were elected for the North West and Yorkshire and Humber regions, respectively. The figures walking towards me down the corridor in Strasbourg were creatures from the political depths, left exposed at low tide as voters deserted the polls.

'For our party to have a grip on the highest but one rung of the electoral ladder,' Griffin had told activists as he launched the party's 2009 election campaign in January, 'would lead to an endless drip-drip of credibility-boosting references to our success in the media. The "wasted vote" chestnut would be well and truly crushed.'[2] Basking in the attention, the week before the European parliament opened, he had made headlines with a couple of choice soundbites. First, he told the BBC that the EU should sink boats carrying migrants from sub-Saharan Africa across the Mediterranean. Then he told Channel 4 News that Islam should be removed from Europe by 'chemotherapy': 'Western values, freedom of speech, democracy and rights for women are incompatible with Islam, which is a cancer eating away at our freedoms and our democracy and rights for our women, and something needs to be done about it.'

Griffin's language might have been designed to shock, but neither of these two themes was unique to the BNP. The parliament elected in 2009 reflected a wave of anti-immigrant and anti-Muslim populism across Europe, and other British parties had played a leading role in ushering this populism towards the mainstream. UKIP had formed the Europe of Freedom and Democracy bloc, partnering with Italy's Northern League – which demands autonomy for northern Italy and has a track record of xenophobic, anti-gay and anti-Islam statements

– along with Danish, Finnish, Greek and Slovak nationalists. Before the election, this had been a fairly moderate grouping of Eurosceptic parties; now it was dominated by anti-immigration sentiment and described by the anti-fascist magazine *Searchlight* as 'far right-lite'. Nikki Sinclaire, a UKIP MEP elected in 2009, resigned from her party a year later, blaming 'extreme views' among UKIP's allies, including 'anti-Semitism, violence and the espousal of a single European policy on immigration'.[3]

They were not alone. Under the direction of David Cameron, the Tories quit the centre-right European People's Party to form a new, Eurosceptic coalition, the European Conservatives and Reformists. Their main partner was Poland's socially conservative Law and Justice party, which has a well-documented record of anti-gay rhetoric. Its leader in the European Parliament, Michal Kaminski, was a member of the far-right, anti-Semitic National Revival of Poland in the late 1980s. In 2001, the US-based Anti-Defamation League accused him of having attempted to stop the commemoration of a wartime pogrom against Jewish people in the Polish town of Jedwabne.[4]

Edward McMillan-Scott, a committed pro-European Tory MEP of twenty-five years, respected across the political divide, was expelled from the Tory group on 15 July 2009 when he stood against Kaminski in an election for vice-president of the parliament. Describing himself to me as a 'loyal Tory', who spent the 1980s working in Poland with reformist groups, McMillan-Scott regretted going against the wishes of his party, but said he was compelled to do so by what he called 'the rise of respectable fascism' in Europe. 'This is where the modern Conservative Party has to tread very carefully,' McMillan-Scott told me. 'David Cameron has done a remarkable job in repositioning the party on most things. Its attitude to gays, or the environment, for example, has fundamentally changed. There's just the question of these links [to right-wing extremists in Europe] and one can't close one's mind to it.'

Griffin's challenge was to make his voice heard above the competition. After the *non-inscrits* meeting finished, I persuaded him to sit down for a brief interview. Within a few moments, it was clear that, even in 2009, his underlying beliefs had not altered. Society was nearing an inevitable 'collapse', most likely prompted by 'peak oil', after which the folly of a multiracial society would be laid bare: 'The simple fact is that wherever you look in history at places where there have been several nations in place, you either find continual outbursts of bloodshed and trouble, or you have a brutal dictatorship compelling them to get along and mix, usually by way of divide and rule, which is obviously why the global businesspeople favour immigration.'

The idea that Britain had benefited from immigration was 'simple racism. You wouldn't dare go to a group of Australian Aborigines or a group of North American Indians and say that they should "celebrate diversity".'

I said I found this an odd position, given the BNP's historical attachment to the British Empire. Does that mean it was wrong for Britain to have colonized Australia, for example? 'Yeah in a certain way it was.' Griffin squirmed a little. 'But it is something which is done, it cannot be undone. History moves on.' He continued, setting out a vision of racial separatism that he has espoused since his days in the National Front: 'The whole of humanity has to find an antidote to globalism. An imperialist or fascist position would be to say we [alone] are entitled to remain separate and to preserve our identity and to have our children growing up like our grandchildren. That would definitely be racism. To say everybody is entitled to their own place and their own space and to preserve that for their own kind and culture, that's a principled position.'

He claimed to hold the same 'principled' position when it came to Islam; by which logic he said he opposed the wars in Afghanistan and Iraq: 'I'm very critical, as you know, of the Islamification of Europe, but I don't believe for one moment that the West has a right to de-Islamify the Middle East. The only possible peace settlement is basically that we leave their sphere of influence for them and they leave our sphere of influence for us.'

This, he summed up with a piece of homespun wisdom: 'Good fences make good neighbours.'

The image of neighbourly propriety was exactly what elected BNP candidates were expected to display among their constituents. Shortly before the 2009 elections, I travelled to meet Alby and Ellie Walker, councillors in the West Midlands town of Stoke-on-Trent, which with nine BNP councillors was described by Griffin as the party's 'jewel in the crown'. Sitting in their shared office, calmly extolling the virtues of hard work and enterprise, the Walkers could have passed for run-of-the-mill Tory councillors, were it not for the slogan reading 'People like you – voting BNP' and anti-Muslim headlines torn from the *Sun* and *Daily Express* newspapers plastered on the walls around them. Alby, the owner of a small joinery firm, even claimed to have been a Conservative voter before he joined the BNP: 'I took Thatcherism on board and set up a company during the year when Thatcher said do it, we'll support small businesses. And it actually worked for me. I supported Margaret Thatcher at the time, I supported the Conservatives, but looking back on that now, I think I was misguided. I think they did a lot of damage to the country through the destruction of industries.'

This view of Thatcher is common in Stoke, a town once famous for its mining and ceramics industries – or 'pits and pots' as they were once respectively known – both of which were devastated during the 1980s. Thanks to a growing disillusionment with the local mainstream parties,[5] the BNP had won support by playing up a range of grievances associated with the town's neglect, campaigning on the closure of local pubs ('enclaves of the English working class, they do not lend themselves to the multi-racial agenda'), or the acute shortage of social housing, which was blamed, falsely, on immigration.[6] As in Dagenham, the BNP had run a neighbourhood 'clean-up' campaign, offering to trim the hedges of elderly residents.

In fact, councillors like the Walkers were rare. One of the most successful anti-BNP propaganda lines was to point out the criminal records of many candidates, or, more simply, their councillors' poor attendance: one effective leaflet distributed in Barking and Dagenham compared expenses claimed with attendance and calculated that each BNP councillor cost the borough £1600 per official meeting.[7] In Stoke, however, the Walkers and a number of their colleagues had learned quickly, making themselves part of their ward's social life by running bingo sessions, or dropping in on the heads of residents' associations once or twice a week with a six-pack of beer.[8] All councillors want to be on good terms with their constituents, but the BNP strategy was to go that one step further. 'Here's my mobile number,' went a familiar refrain, reported by community activists I met in several towns. 'Any time you need me, I'll be there.'[9] What would being 'there' mean in practice?

* * *

Number 555-557 Uttoxeter Road in Stoke, once home to Habib Khan and his family, is easy to spot. For a start, it's twice as large as all the other houses on the street; a pair of semis knocked through. If that doesn't get your attention, then the Grecian columns and amphora-shaped garden ornaments probably will. In 2001, Khan, a kebab shop owner and respected member of Stoke's small Muslim community had mentioned to Keith Brown, a former colleague from a Stoke ceramics firm, that he was looking to buy a house. Brown offered to pass his details on to the owner of two empty properties next door to his home on Uttoxeter Road; Khan ended up buying them. Initially, relations between the new neighbours were cordial, but the friendship soured when in 2003 Khan, whose business was prospering, decided to renovate his houses. Brown tried unsuccessfully to block the planning application and the dispute festered, with Brown's anger focusing on builders' use of a shared driveway between the houses. When Khan attempted reconciliation, he was rebuffed, Brown allegedly telling him 'my house is old, your house is new, I don't like it.'[10]

In search of support, Brown contacted his local councillor, a BNP member, in May 2003. There was little practical help the BNP could offer with the dispute, but Brown was increasingly drawn into the party's orbit. As Michael Coleman, another BNP councillor contacted by Brown explained, 'I got talking to him about politics and we found he agreed with the politics of the BNP. He . . . became a key activist.'[11] As Brown and his son became active supporters of the BNP, helping deliver leaflets for the party's election campaigns, the neighbours' dispute took on a racist element. According to Khan's eldest son Khazir Saddique, 'We used to get called Pakis and told we can't live here. We had our windows smashed every day. They made it as hard as they could for us. It was just a nightmare.'[12]

On 6 July 2007, Khan was inside his house when a fight broke out between his son and members of Brown's family. Grabbing a kitchen knife, Khan ran outside and in the resulting altercation stabbed Keith Brown in the back, killing him. A year later, Khan was sentenced to eight years in prison for manslaughter, the judge acknowledging that the incident came after years of racist abuse from Brown and his son.[13]

Perhaps you can guess what happened next: the BNP, gifted with an opportunity to create a white martyr, used the killing to whip up hostility against Muslims in Stoke. Griffin attended Brown's funeral, along with a BNP film crew, and Simon Darby, the BNP's deputy leader, blogged daily from the courtroom during the trial. When the verdict – manslaughter – was announced in May 2008, Coleman told reporters on the steps of the court, 'we advise anybody who gets angry, get involved with the BNP'.[14] A rally for BNP activists from across the country was announced for later that summer.

The target of the propaganda, however, was not Muslims directly, but the supposedly corrupt political establishment who, the BNP argued, had allowed this killing to happen. Coleman, the BNP councillor who had befriended Brown, led a campaign for 'justice' in the pages of the *Stoke Sentinel*.[15] Brown's widow, Julia Barker, was persuaded to make a formal complaint against the police, alleging that Brown had been the victim of political correctness, with police doing nothing to protect the white family against abuse from Khan. When investigators from the Independent Police Complaints Commission attempted to interview Julia Barker, they found their way blocked by the BNP. Ms Barker could not be interviewed directly because of 'health concerns', they were told; instead, BNP councillors would make representations on her behalf.[16] At the same time, Barker was being coached to give an interview to the BNP's 'alternative' media operation BNPtv, which was then distributed online and by DVD in order to drum up support.

At the rally, held in a car park along one of the main roads into the centre of Stoke, senior BNP figures from the town including Alby Walker and Michael Coleman stood alongside Griffin, who railed against the 'establishment, by which I mean the police, the courts, the newspaper editors, the people who run the BBC and the fat cat politicians at local and national level.'[17]

At heart, this was the old Rights for Whites tactic, but now the BNP had an official platform in local government from which to spread their propaganda. Avoiding the crudest form of racist sloganeering, the BNP linked the killing with a wider political discontent felt by many of the town's residents. 'If whites attack their coloured neighbours,' Griffin continued, 'they are criminal scumbags as well . . . all we are asking for is fair play for our people. Ignoring our people, ignoring our rights, pretending we do not exist is no longer an option.'

Griffin may have insisted that the BNP's campaign over the Keith Brown killing had nothing to do with Habib Khan's race or religion. But behind this anti-establishment positioning, councillors in Stoke were also using their positions to encourage distrust of the town's Muslims. They opposed plans to build new mosques, attempting to block one planning application in 2008 on the grounds that the call to prayer would 'provoke neighbours'. Coleman, who gained a further position of responsibility when he was elected governor of a Stoke secondary school, tried to drum up support for a campaign against the provision of halal meat in the city's schools. This posturing was willingly relayed by local media – perhaps understandably, since the town was being run by a power-sharing coalition of Labour, Lib Dems and Conservatives, and the BNP were the only political opposition to speak of.

The anti-Muslim campaigns had a wider resonance. A decade earlier, the Tyndall-era BNP had distributed a leaflet that railed against the perceived savagery of kosher slaughter; fortunately it was of interest to virtually no one, instantly recognizable as anti-Semitic propaganda.[18] Fast forward ten years, replace the word 'kosher' with the word 'halal', and the BNP would find a much more receptive audience. The fall-out from the War on Terror, and the aftermath of the 2005 London bombings, had already fuelled the BNP's propaganda, but by 2008 Britain's fear of terrorism was morphing into a generalized antipathy to 'foreign' Muslim culture.

In January that year, the Archbishop of Canterbury made a speech that was widely misinterpreted as a call for Britain to adopt sharia law, drawing stinging criticism from the right-wing press. The same month, Bishop Michael Nazir-Ali warned of Muslim self-imposed segregation and claimed that parts of the UK had become 'no go areas' for non-Muslims. In March, a Christian think tank published a report, based on questionable statistics, suggesting that the number of mosques would soon overtake churches. Together, these three strands combined into an overriding theme, shared by tabloids and broadsheets alike: that Islam was threatening to overwhelm native British culture; a fear summed up by headlines such as 'Islam set to be top religion; mosques to beat churches' (*Daily Star*, 26 March); 'More attending mosques than mass by 2020' (*Daily Express*, 26

March); 'Muslims will soon outnumber traditional churchgo-
ers' (*Daily Telegraph*, 25 March); 'Britain to turn Islamic by
2035' (*Daily Star*, 9 May). According to an extensive study of
press coverage of Muslims conducted by academics at Cardiff
University, 2008 was the year in which the number of stories
about the religious and cultural differences of Muslims over-
took those about Islamist-inspired terrorism.[19]

This was a fertile environment for the BNP, enabling it to
link the sense of grievance it had cultivated with a more general
hostility to Muslims. In January 2008, the *Daily Express*
published a photo in support of Nazir-Ali's comments about
no-go areas, which featured several women in face veils, one of
whom was sticking two fingers up at the photographer. The
BNP turned this into a widely distributed leaflet in Stoke,
setting it alongside a photograph of pottery kilns taken during
the city's industrial heyday. A similar leaflet was distributed in
London during the 2008 London mayoral elections, which saw
the Dagenham BNP councillor, Richard Barnbrook, elected to
the London Assembly.

By the time Griffin made his parliamentary debut in Strasbourg,
this growing hostility towards Islam had provoked a new development. On 10 March 2009, soldiers from the Royal Anglian
regiment staged a homecoming parade in Luton. A small group
of young men linked to the extremist Muslim sect Islam4UK
demonstrated against them, shouting 'terrorists' and holding
up placards that read 'Anglian soldiers go to hell'. This provoked
an angry reaction from members of the crowd, some of whom
began attacking Asians. Later that evening the mayor of Luton
– a Sikh – was kicked to the ground by a young white man.[20]
The ensuing press coverage focused almost exclusively on the

actions of Islam4UK, following the usual pattern of blurring the distinction between a tiny group of publicity-hungry fanatics and mainstream Muslim opinion. Several weeks later, an anti-Muslim street protest took place in Luton, gathering supporters via the local football hooligan 'firms'. A second march ended with Asian-owned shops being attacked. Further demonstrations were announced that summer and the movement acquired a name: the English Defence League.

Since the vicious split with Combat 18 in the mid-90s, the BNP had avoided overt links with any far-right street movement. Now, one had sprung up independently, it seemed, and it was growing rapidly. The English Defence League provided an outlet for the kind of adrenaline-pumping street politics that often attracts people to the far right; a world away from cutting old ladies' hedges and picking up litter. What's more, in focusing exclusively on Islamic 'extremism', it appeared to have an appeal much more suited to the realities of modern Britain. The BNP's efforts to seem non-racist were always unconvincing, not least to the party's own activists. By contrast, the EDL had a strategic advantage in picking a single issue – and one primarily of religion, rather than race. A Sikh man, Guramit Singh, emerged as a spokesperson for the movement and one early EDL slogan was stolen directly from the anti-racist movement of the 1970s: 'black and white unite'.

Even if the BNP leadership remained hostile, with Griffin condemning the new movement as an MI5 plot,[21] a number of lower-level BNP activists were soon identified as having roles in organizing the EDL. This was bad news for Griffin. Despite the European election victories, the BNP's progress had been stalling, partly as a result of increased campaigning by anti-fascist groups, but also because of internal conflicts. In

December 2007, the party's group development manager, Sadie Graham, was sacked after she raised concerns over financial irregularities. In 2008 her supporters mounted a leadership challenge, which was only halted by a complex set of rules designed by Griffin to make it difficult for opponents to gather enough nomination signatures.

The episode took its toll on morale and the party lost several hundred members: at a meeting in 2008, Griffin was told that the dispute had adversely affected the BNP's capacity to build local branches and groups.[22] In response to flagging spirits, readers of *Identity* were begged to 'keep shoving those leaflets through doors' in an article titled 'Depression: our greatest enemy'.

In the autumn of 2009, however, Griffin was offered his greatest opportunity yet – by the BBC.

9

Political Correctness Gone Mad

On the afternoon of 22 October 2009, an angry crowd gathered outside BBC television centre in West London. At around twenty past five, as several hundred protesters chanted 'shame on you BBC' and strained against police barriers, Nick Griffin quietly entered the building by a side door. Once inside, he was ushered through to a sound stage where, shortly before seven in the evening, recording would begin on that week's episode of *Question Time*.

With a prime-time slot on BBC1, *Question Time* is the BBC's most popular current affairs programme. Members of the audience ask topical questions to a panel comprised of politicians, writers and other members of the country's elite. Debate is shallow; rather it is an opportunity to trade soundbites, or to beam a little light demagoguery into the living rooms of Britain. What so incensed the anti-fascist demonstrators outside Television Centre was that it was on exactly this kind of programme that Jean-Marie le Pen had made his first step into France's political mainstream in 1984.[1] The BBC pleaded that its hands were tied, arguing that strict impartiality rules gave it, in the words of director general Mark Thompson, 'an obligation to scrutinize and hold to account all elected representatives'. But the quest for ratings also played its part. As James Macintyre, a former *Question Time* producer revealed in the *New Statesman*, the programme makers had been pushing for Griffin's inclusion since 2007, knowing that the furore caused by his presence would draw in viewers.[2] *Question Time* was Punch and Judy politics at its height.

Ranged against the BNP leader were Baroness Sayeeda Warsi, the Tories' shadow community cohesion minister, the Lib Dem MP Chris Huhne and the black American writer Bonnie Greer. The question of whether the government should put anyone up against Griffin had split the cabinet, with the Welsh Secretary Peter Hain and the Home Secretary Alan Johnson arguing forcefully at a meeting on 15 September that Labour should maintain its policy of 'no platform' for fascists. But they were in a minority, and twelve days later, the Justice Secretary Jack Straw was chosen as the final panellist.[3]

Within minutes of the programme starting, however, it was clear Griffin had fluffed it. In 1984, Le Pen had delivered a frighteningly charismatic performance, wrong-footing his opponents by insisting at the start on a minute's silence 'for Stalin's victims of the Gulag'. There were no such grand gestures from Griffin: he rambled, prevaricated, seemed unable to give straight answers to straight questions. When the subject of Holocaust denial was raised, he had a strange smirk on his face. As one BNP member later put it, Griffin put in 'a shameful performance which allowed the party to be portrayed as of low-grade political acumen'. Viewers 'tuned in expecting to see a lion, instead they saw a mouse'.[4] Above all, his views on race were so obviously out of step with the Britain reflected in the audience. As one Asian man challenged: 'Where do you want me to go? This is my country. I love this country. I was born here. I was educated here. You'd be surprised how many people would have a whip-round to buy you a ticket to go to the South Pole, it's a colourless landscape. You'd love it.'

But if Griffin's own performance was lacking, his very presence threw the failings of contemporary politics into sharp relief. The most emotive subject on the programme was the BNP's manipulation of Britain's war legacy: images of Winston Churchill and Second World War iconography abounded on BNP propaganda. War and death are often the founding stones of national identity, and Jack Straw argued forcefully for the inclusion of black and Asian Britons in this most sensitive area with an anecdote about the bodies of young white Lancashire soldiers lying side-by-side with Indians in a First World War graveyard. But what about the current wars, in Iraq and Afghanistan, of which he was a key supporter? And what of the perceived 'enemy within', British Muslims? It was in Straw's own constituency of Blackburn that the BNP had won a council seat partly by spreading the false rumour of the plan to recreate Saddam Hussein's giant arch of crossed swords. And Straw himself had started a 'debate' in 2006 when he gave an interview saying that he asked Muslim women to remove their face veils during his constituency surgeries. Griffin's assertion that Islam did not 'fit in with the fundamental values of British democracy: free speech, democracy and equal rights for women' drew some applause from the *Question Time* audience.

On the question of immigration, the representatives of all three main parties wavered. Jack Straw praised Britain's 'long history' of ethnic diversity – taking care to point out that it was not Labour but a Tory Government who had brought people from the Caribbean to work in the NHS in 1960 – but had to be pressed by the show's presenter David Dimbleby on whether current immigration policies were encouraging support for the

BNP. Chris Huhne made an unconvincing attempt to sound tough on the subject.

Sayeeda Warsi, widely regarded as the heroine of the night for her acknowledgement that the success of the BNP was not about race but 'resources', and that 'the mainstream parties have a responsibility to tackle the underlying issues' was hamstrung by her own party's policy, promising a cap on immigration when she knew full well that it could not apply to the majority of immigrants, who came from within the EU. And Warsi herself had once succumbed to the race-to-the-bottom politics the BNP so often provoked. 'Are you thinking of voting BNP? Think again,' leaflets for Warsi's 2005 campaign for parliament had declared. 'If you vote BNP you are allowing Labour to creep in with more political correctness and uncontrolled immigration and asylum.'[5] In the midst of a global recession, the real question of 'resources' was barely touched upon.

Question Time did not give Griffin the feared boost in the opinion polls. It was a relief, but it also let the rest of the panel off the hook: they represented a tarnished political class, whose own disconnect from the public had led them into a squabble over issues that could have long since been dead and buried. Before them, in the audience, was living, breathing evidence of Britain's everyday multiculturalism. And beyond the studio lights, stood a silent mass of voters whose interests were not being adequately represented. The BNP may have sought to twist the 'four concepts' of liberal democracy to their own ends, but what did they stand for in modern British politics? Freedom – for bankers? Security – at the expense of Muslims? Identity – as a substitute for class? Democracy?

What's more, in a letter to *The Times*, the former *Sunday Telegraph* editor Peregrine Worsthorne reminded Britain of its not-so distant past. 'In considering whether a racist should be allowed a seat on *Question Time*,' he wrote, a few days before the broadcast 'it is chastening to remember that most of my octogenarian generation of British, high as well as low, believed in white superiority . . . As it happens, I am no longer a racist, but the arguments that made me one in the relatively recent past still do not seem to me to be so abhorrent as to be out of order in civilised debate. Unquestionably, the leader of the BNP – an unsavoury character – is not the right man to do such arguments justice, but that is because of his bigotry rather than the views themselves.'[6]

Would Griffin's comment the following day, that it was unfair to stage *Question Time* in central London because the city had been 'ethnically cleansed', have any resonance? With the BNP's public profile at an all-time high, a general election was only seven months away. In mid-November, Griffin announced he would be standing for parliament against Margaret Hodge in Barking.

As gap-year activities go, canvassing for the BNP is not on most teenagers' wish-lists, but eighteen-year-old George was an exception. With his public school quiff and Union Jack tie, and armed with a clipboard, he was spending this Saturday afternoon in April 2010 working his way along the streets of the Becontree estate. George, and his canvassing partner Phil, a thirty-four-year-old mental health worker from Lincoln, had answered a nationwide call for BNP activists to try to help the party gain its first ever Member of Parliament. This was only the tip of the party's biggest ever general election effort, standing a record 338 candidates across the country. It was in Barking that Griffin judged he had the best chance of winning – still an unlikely prospect, but a valuable publicity boost, particularly as local elections, in which the BNP was standing over 700 candidates, were to be held on the same day. Immigration had emerged as a dominant theme of the 2010 elections; a fact not lost on BNP activists. 'The rhetoric of the *Express* and the *Mail* could come from one of our own newsletters,' George told me. 'But then they have to say: "Don't vote for those fascists!" It's ridiculous.'

In a neat cul-de-sac, two men in their thirties were sitting on the front step of a house, catching the afternoon sun. 'Is it true the BNP want to get rid of all the Gurkhas?' one of them asked, referring to the retired Nepalese soldiers who had recently been granted the right to settle in the UK. 'No,' George replied. 'In fact, our chairman Nick Griffin said he'd gladly replace 100,000 British-born Muslims with 100,000 loyal Gurkhas who fought for this country.' The man looked impressed. 'Yeah, I'd go for that.'

Back on the main road, George and Phil were given a shout of support from a man across the street: 'You're doing a good job, boys! Get rid of all those niggers.' A black mother and her two daughters who were walking past at that moment quickened their pace. George and Phil exchanged an awkward look. 'He's probably had a bit too much to drink,' George said.

Later that afternoon, in the back garden of the nearby Cherry Tree pub, Griffin officially launched his campaign for parliament. His face-off with Hodge, dubbed the 'battle for Barking' by journalists, was one of the big stories of the 2010 election, and the BNP had done its best to drum up a sense of occasion as reporters and television news crews from around the world gathered. Griffin posed by the party's advertising bus – the 'Truth Truck' – which had been driving around the constituency all morning, piping Gilbert and Sullivan through the tannoy, interspersed with pleas to vote BNP. At the pub, party activists busied themselves organizing the afternoon's canvassing while Griffin's wife collected empties and joked with supporters. The garden-party atmosphere was only spoiled when a member of the security team began showing me a choke hold he'd used on a *Times* journalist ejected from a BNP press conference earlier in the year. He was swiftly ushered away by a press officer.

But by April 2010, the wheels were coming off the BNP's campaign. Since the European elections, the party had come under intense pressure from within and without. In the summer of 2009, the Equalities and Human Rights Commission launched legal proceedings against the BNP over its constitution, which banned non-whites from joining the party. The court case rumbled on throughout the winter of 2009–2010; a drain on energy and resources, during which time the party was banned from recruiting any more members. Although the case ended in a stalemate, with both sides claiming victory (the BNP altered the wording of its constitution; the new wording was then ruled 'indirectly discriminatory'), it exacerbated tensions between hardline activists and those who saw the strategic need to accept non-white members.[7] As Griffin warned his party in September 2009, it was time for the BNP to 'adapt or die'.

To compound matters, a kind of malaise had overtaken the BNP since the 2009 European elections. Rather than inspire activists, the success had provoked complacency. According to Eddy Butler, who was now in charge of election strategy, there grew 'a strange attitude that people thought, "job done".' He explained: 'It's a recurring phenomenon, because my sort of politics is starved of success . . . When others win something, they want to win the next one. They get on a roll. It's the opposite way round in the BNP.'

One indication of this falling momentum was that the BNP had trouble getting enough council candidates to stand in Barking and Dagenham, the very borough where its support was strongest. Although its opponents had feared the party might win overall control, it could only muster thirty-four candidates for a possible fifty-one seats.[8]

What's more, internal discontent at Griffin's leadership had not dissipated since the failed challenge in 2008. In particular, attention focused on the relationship between Griffin and a forty-five-year-old businessman named Jim Dowson. Based in Northern Ireland but originally from Scotland, Dowson was a hardline Protestant anti-abortion campaigner and ex-member of the Orange Order who convinced Griffin that he could professionalize the BNP's operations. Dowson began by organizing fundraising appeals but his role soon expanded to cover a revamp of the party's administration, establishing a base for the party in Belfast. An investigation by the anti-fascist magazine *Searchlight* in 2010 reported that Dowson 'practically owned' the party.[9]

Griffin admitted to me that Dowson 'did piss people off', but claimed that without his advice on how to 'professionalize' campaigning, the BNP would never have won seats in the European Parliament. He put discontent at Dowson down to 'the strain of turning [the BNP] from a volunteer organization into a disciplined one where you actually have people expected to clock in and out and fill certain roles and targets like a business'. He went on: 'You're working with volunteers who have sacrificed a lot. The movement's a litter of wrecked marriages and broken families and the rest of it, because of the pressure put on them. And when they're suddenly told just having a title and doing a bit isn't enough, you've got to meet these targets and all the rest of it, it's an enormous strain.'

According to Butler, however, party activists were also disgruntled at Griffin's increasingly aloof behaviour. One attraction of having seats in the European Parliament was the thousands of pounds in expenses they would bring, but EU rules on how the money can be spent are strict, and BNP activists who had expected to be given jobs after the 2009 election were disappointed when these did not materialize. Instead of dealing with the issue, says Butler, Griffin withdrew: 'He cut himself off and wouldn't talk to anyone suddenly. He went from being ridiculously over accessible to being under accessible. Which pissed people off who thought they had his private [phone] number. You couldn't get a single decision out of him. You could never pin him down to sit and talk. Then you'd have to go through this Dowson guy, who wasn't one of us.'

A few days after I met the BNP canvassers, I was back on Becontree, this time watching Margaret Hodge dashing between doorstep conversations, each of which she began with a bright 'Hello, I'm your MP'. Since 2006, Barking and Dagenham's housing crisis had not gone away: at the time I visited, there were 11,695 families on the waiting list, and local anger was still being directed at the new faces on the street. As I followed Hodge, complaints about housing cropped up again and again. We heard tales of families that had been made to wait three, five or even more years to get a home. One man had spent eight years living in a one-bedroom flat with his wife and four children. A young mother said she was considering voting BNP because she liked the party's insistence that 'local people get local housing'. She added hurriedly: 'I'm not racist, though – half my family are black.' Hodge turned to me and grimaced, as if to say: 'You see what we're up against?'

But there had been a change: Hodge and her team were listening to the outpouring of anti-immigrant feeling, then – and this was something of a departure for a New Labour politician – calmly explaining that the housing shortage had been caused by the Right to Buy scheme and Labour's failure to build more homes. Only in 2009 did the government change the law to allow councils to reinvest money collected from rent in house-building programmes.

Since 2006 Hodge had made a concerted effort to turn around Labour's fortunes in her constituency. She moved her office here from Westminster and oversaw measures to rejuvenate the local party and boost recruitment. Several councillors were deselected and the party took on a wave of younger, more ethnically diverse members to reflect the borough's changing demographics. Taking a cue from Lancashire, where the Burnley BNP had already been driven back by a rejuvenated Liberal Democrat branch, Barking Labour redoubled its efforts to engage with the public, holding coffee mornings, street meetings and distributing newsletters. Most importantly, it knocked on doors, just like the BNP had done by 'stealth', five years previously. While Labour's contact rate – the proportion of houses in a constituency visited by canvassers – was a measly 7 per cent in 2006, by May 2010 it had reached 62 per cent.[10] Across the constituency border, Dagenham's MP Jon Cruddas had made similar efforts, and between them, the party had identified around 20,000 Labour voters who could potentially turn out on polling day. This pointed to how the BNP could be beaten: not by pandering to their agenda, but by targeting the much larger group of potential Labour voters who had previously abstained.

Despite all this, Hodge was still playing the 'triangulation' game. In February 2010, she argued that migrants should be made to wait up to twelve months before they could get access to the benefits system. 'The left don't like what I've been saying,' she conceded. 'But I think you can puncture racism by dealing with the feeling of unfairness that people have.' Hadn't her statements – particularly given the dominance of anti-immigration newspapers – simply encouraged racism? 'Politicians always shy away from talking about immigration and the difficult issues that are associated with it. If we don't address those issues, we allow that territory to be captured by the extreme right,' Hodge said. She accepted that 'both main political parties should have invested far more in affordable social housing much sooner,' and then added, 'but social housing is not universal, it is something that has to be rationed, and socialism has always been about the language of priorities.'

Nationally, neither Labour nor the Tories' campaigns were completely free from the taint of racism. In the Romford constituency of Andrew Rosindell, the Tory spokesman on home affairs, Conservative Party leaflets were distributed claiming that Labour had opened the 'floodgates' to immigration and demanded that 'foreign criminals' be removed from Britain.[11] This was swiftly condemned as 'dog whistle politics' by Labour's immigration minister Phil Woolas, but it later emerged that Woolas himself, frightened of losing his seat in Oldham East, was advised by his team to adopt a 'get the white vote angry' strategy. Woolas issued leaflets implying that his Lib Dem rival was courting support from Islamic extremists.[12]

Even Labour's 2010 election manifesto carried a section titled 'crime and immigration', as if the two were intimately linked.

Hodge's team knocked at another door. The white-haired man in his fifties who answered said he'd vote for 'whoever is going to stop all this immigration. I drive a bus, and no one on it speaks English any more.'

'Well, they *all* should speak English,' Hodge replied.

Fortunately, the anti-BNP campaign in 2010 did not begin and end with New Labour. Hope not Hate, launched by *Searchlight* in 2005 as a 'positive antidote' to the BNP's message, was supported by several major trade unions and the *Mirror* newspaper. It had employed Blue State Digital, the US online agency that had helped Barack Obama win the presidency in 2008, to compile what it claimed was Britain's biggest political email list. With 142,000 supporters across the UK, it was able to mobilize activists to deliver leaflets, or canvass by telephone in areas threatened by the BNP. On 17 April, Hope not Hate supporters delivered 91,000 anti-BNP newspapers – what it claimed was the largest political mobilization of the 2010 general election campaign.[13]

The smaller organization Unite Against Fascism, backed again by trade unions, was also active, staging a Love Music Hate Racism concert in Stoke-on-Trent to a 20,000-strong audience. Hundreds of members leafleted in target areas across the country, warning voters of the BNP's Nazi heritage and the violent history of its members.

As Sam Tarry, a Hope not Hate campaigner and Labour council candidate for Barking and Dagenham, explained to me, the aim was to turn the BNP into a 'toxic brand'. Leaflets either targeted unpleasant aspects of BNP behaviour – a candidate's insulting comments about the death of David Cameron's disabled son; the party's failure to support the England football team because black players were 'not British' – or warned people about the effects a BNP-controlled council would have on local investment.

Campaigners also focused on boosting turnout among ethnic minorities: a community organizer was appointed to liaise with congregations at African churches in Barking and Dagenham. And, Tarry explained, the most productive routes involved working through some decidedly Old Labour organizations: 'The volume of trade union members in the borough is remarkably high – as if Thatcher and the coal miners never happened – so when we analysed the BNP vote, it was clear that a significant proportion of local trade unionists must have voted for them. We put out messages about why the BNP are anti-worker, and brought people from African churches together in meetings with the mainly white trade unionists. That was so they could recruit people from those churches into the trade union, so that the anxiety about wages being depressed [by immigration] was undermined, because you have people being recruited into a trade union all on the same side, as it were.'

Both Hope not Hate and UAF's campaigns were a rejoinder to the pessimists who believed Britain was 'sleepwalking' into segregation, irrevocably divided by religion, culture or race. Once again, it was grassroots action that confronted the far right.

As election day approached, the pressure was taking its toll on the BNP. Thanks to Dowson's fundraising techniques, the party had gathered the £300,000 required for deposits, but it relied on promises from Griffin of major breakthroughs in Stoke-on-Trent and Barking and Dagenham, hugely raising members' expectations.[14] Its campaign was officially launched on 23 April – St George's Day – by a man dressed up as a Crusader. But, inexplicably, given that the aim was to attract media attention, the event took place in Stoke-on-Trent, rather than London. Campaign material lacked focus and BNP leaflets increasingly concentrated on attacking Hope not Hate, rather than putting forward the party's own policies.[15]

What's more, the campaign had further alienated party activists from the leadership. Griffin's habit of imposing himself and other senior BNP figures as candidates in seats with high BNP support had been causing friction since the start of his leadership. Richard Barnbrook, the party's sole representative on the London Assembly, who had stood for parliament in Barking in 2005 and come third, had assumed he would stand again, and was furious when he was told to stand aside.[16] In the West Midlands, Alby Walker had expected to be chosen as candidate for Stoke Central, given his local media profile. When he was passed over in favour of the BNP's deputy leader Simon Darby, Walker quit the party and ran as an independent, doing his best to damage the BNP's election campaign by claiming its members still had 'Nazi-esque' tendencies and revealing that prospective candidates were given media training on how to avoid questions about the Holocaust.[17] The BNP could only muster six council candidates out of a possible twenty in Stoke.

As election day neared, tempers frayed. Butler was sacked from his party job in March, while over the Easter weekend, disputes over money came to a head when the BNP's publicity director, Mark Collett, was arrested on suspicion of making death threats against Dowson and Griffin, who in turn accused him of plotting a 'palace coup'. (Collett was questioned, but not charged.) On the day before polling day, the BNP's webmaster took the party website offline – the fallout from a publicity stunt that had backfired,[18] while the BNP's group leader on Barking and Dagenham council, Bob Bailey, was filmed by a BBC news crew fighting in the street with a group of Asian men.

When the results came in, they signalled a rout. The BNP lost all but two of the twenty-eight council seats it was defending and was completely wiped out on Barking and Dagenham council. In the parliamentary election, Griffin received a lower vote share, 14.6 per cent, than the BNP had done in 2005. It seemed the BNP had suffered a repeat of the fate that befell the National Front in 1979, which had stood a record number of candidates, but had over-stretched and collapsed.

Griffin tried to put a positive spin on the results, claiming that the party had 'spectacularly tripled its vote from 2005', ignoring the fact that it had contested nearly three times as many seats. He blamed Labour 'gerrymandering through immigration' for the Barking and Dagenham defeat, and an 'underdeveloped elections department' – which was a pre-emptive attack on Eddy Butler, around whom Griffin's opponents were gathering for a possible leadership challenge. Butler, for his part, called for members to 'stick in there and build a new future'. The BNP needed 'a leadership which is a bonus and a credit to our Party in the eyes of the public and not a downward drag on our vote'.[19]

While opponents celebrated, one stark fact remained: the BNP's vote had gone up.

Its best results were in or nearby former industrial areas, away from the inner cities: on the outer fringes of London, in North West England, parts of the North East and the West Midlands, as well as a few South Wales constituencies.[20] With 564,331 votes, or 1.9 per cent of the total (as compared to 0.74 per cent in 2005), it was now 'the fifth largest party in the United

Kingdom', according to the political scientist Vernon Bogdanor. Its candidates averaged a higher number of votes each than they had done in 2005. As Bogdanor pointed out, 'in the 1930s, in the midst of a depression, when educational and living standards were far lower, Mosley's Fascists failed to win a single council seat, and were unable to put up candidates in the general election of 1935. The BNP is doing far better.'[21] Even if the party was on the verge of collapse, its support was not.

On the afternoon of 5 March 2010, I was standing on the steps of Tate Britain – just downriver from the Houses of Parliament – amid a crowd of perturbed onlookers. We were watching several hundred English Defence League supporters gather behind a police cordon, preparing to march the few hundred yards up the road to the House of Lords. For the most part, the crowd could have come from any far-right street rally at any point over the last few decades: predominantly male and aggressive, the crowd were chanting offensive slogans and taunting passers-by who stopped to remonstrate. Using a loud hailer, one of the group was attempting to whip his fellow demonstrators into a frenzy, with a rant that climaxed by demanding that a minority group 'burn in fucking hell'.

But something here was different: the speaker was Asian – a Sikh, by religion – and although there were few other non-white faces in the crowd, his words were warmly received. Others held up placards bearing the Star of David and the slogan 'We support Israel'; one man wore a pink triangle on his clothing, the symbol homosexuals were forced to wear in Nazi concentration camps, and held aloft a sign that proclaimed lesbian, gay, bi and transsexual solidarity. What's more, the EDL – which describes itself as a 'human rights organisation'[22] that takes 'an actively anti-racist and anti-fascist stance' – was demonstrating in support of the right to 'free speech' of Geert Wilders, a Dutch politician who was visiting the UK after initially being banned from entering. What on earth was going on? Surely this, to borrow a favoured phrase of the right, was political correctness gone mad?

As the BNP careened towards disaster in the 2010 general election, the English Defence League was in the ascendant. It appeared to be a new type of far-right movement, co-ordinated online via discussion forums and social networking sites. Grouped into militaristic regional 'divisions', and led by a dozen shadowy figures, who for the most part preferred to stay anonymous or hide behind pseudonyms, it boasted 79,000 'supporters' on Facebook, although this didn't necessarily translate into real-life activists. In over thirty street demonstrations, the EDL had shown it could mobilize up to 3,000 people, the majority drawn from pre-existing networks of football hooligans.[23] It could operate quickly, announcing 'flash' demonstrations online only a few hours before they were to take place.

How had the movement grown so quickly, from a local outburst of anti-Muslim feeling in Luton in the spring of 2009? It began when Stephen Yaxley-Lennon, a former BNP member and organizer of the 'United People of Luton' demonstration, was approached by Alan Ayling, a Christian fundamentalist who went by the alias 'Alan Lake'. Ayling was a wealthy director of a City investment fund, Pacific Capital Management,[24] who had made extensive contacts with anti-Muslim ideologues around the world through his 'counter-jihad' 4Freedoms website and was searching for a UK-based street group which could act as a pressure group to force Islam up the political agenda. 'You can blog and write letters to your MP as much as you like,' Ayling would later state. 'Your MP doesn't care, he doesn't care what you say. The only thing that is going to make people care again, that is our nobility, our elite leaders, is if we have more numbers, and if we sometimes get out on the street.'[25]

In May 2009, Yaxley-Lennon visited Ayling's flat in London's exclusive Barbican district, along with others including the anti-Muslim blogger Paul Ray and Ann Marchini, a north London property investor.[26] Here, they discussed the formation of the English Defence League. Most beneficial to Ayling's cause would be a group that gave the impression of spontaneity; one that adopted the outward trappings of multi-ethnic Britain and could not be pinned down by the accusations of racism and fascism that had hindered the BNP. Although Yaxley-Lennon had previously been a member of the BNP, Ayling insisted that the EDL immediately dissociate itself from the party.[27] It was proposed that Yaxley-Lennon adopt a pseudonym; in this guise he would appear as a media figurehead for the EDL, positioning himself as an authentic voice from the street. The idea of a white working class wronged by the evils of multiculturalism already had great currency in British political life – so who better to carry the EDL's message than an angry young everyman who went by the name 'Tommy Robinson'?

None of this was entirely new. Griffin had been trying to give the BNP an inclusive sheen as far back as the 'ethnic liaison committee' of 2001. (Since then the BNP had attracted a handful of Jewish members, and an election broadcast in 2005 had been delivered by a Sikh.) But the EDL had two clear advantages: first, it was not a formal political party. This meant there were no manifestos, no formal programme that could be seized on by opponents as evidence of the group's true nature. Second, it was a single-issue movement, whose proclaimed enemy was 'radical Islam'. This meant the EDL could more convincingly welcome non-white supporters into its ranks; Yaxley-Lennon even claims to have become disillusioned with the BNP because the party wouldn't let his black friends join.[28] Beyond this, however, familiar factors appear to be driving support: one survey of EDL sympathizers found them to be 'characterised by intense pessimism about the UK's future, worries about immigration and joblessness. This is often mixed with a proactive pride in Britain, British history and British values, which they see as being under attack from Islam.'[29]

The EDL boasts neither a manifesto nor a political programme. Despite the name 'English' Defence League, its website and official communications have next to nothing to say about English identity. Indeed, it's the very ambiguity of 'Englishness' that allows the EDL to operate. While British identity is tied to the state, and there have been a number of official attempts, however successful, to promote an inclusive notion of Britishness, for many people 'English' remains an ethnic category. This was certainly so for the creator of *Midsomer Murders*, a popular rural detective TV series, when he said in March 2011 that the programme could not feature black faces because it was 'the last bastion of Englishness'. Several months later, the comedian John Cleese suggested that English identity was incompatible with cultural diversity, when he claimed in an interview that London was 'no longer an English city', thanks to immigration. Even in football, where the inclusion of Afro-Caribbean players in the England team has done much to undermine racism, Asians are notably absent.

Instead, the group is defined entirely by what it opposes, fixating on issues that have a visceral appeal. The EDL claims to be defending the honour of British soldiers fighting in Afghanistan and it has held demonstrations at Wootton Bassett, the Wiltshire market town through which the coffins of soldiers killed abroad passed until 2011. It plays on the same fear of Muslim sexual deviancy that the BNP tried to exploit, with the commonly used chant 'Allah is a paedo' and protests over the 'grooming' of white girls by Asian men. The 'politically correct' liberal elite is a frequent target of EDL anger, as was the case in December 2010 when Yaxley-Lennon threatened to 'close down' towns whose councils 'banned' the word Christmas. Above all, pickets against the construction of new mosques and against restaurants that serve halal food cast Islam – the religion of several million British citizens – as an invading ideology. Yaxley-Lennon himself displays an abject fear of the growth of Britain's Muslim population: 'Three per cent are Muslim and look at the chaos . . . imagine what happens if they reach 20 per cent, oh my God.'[30]

Death, sex, betrayal, and a 'foreign' intruder: such elements are the building blocks of fascist propaganda. Yet unlike the BNP's commitment to the 'restoration' of a racially pure Britain, Islamophobia has mainstream credibility. It is a prejudice that has 'passed the dinner table test' according to the Conservative peer Sayeeda Warsi. Anti-Islam sentiment has been echoed by politicians, including Labour's Jack Straw, who claimed in January 2011 that some Asian men saw white girls as 'easy meat' for abuse, and the Prime Minister David Cameron, who followed his German and French counterparts in February 2011 by announcing that Islamist terrorism proved that state multi-culturalism had 'failed'. Geert Wilders, the Dutch politician whom, as I had seen, the EDL had taken to the streets to support, had been invited to Britain to screen his anti-Islam film *Fitna* by Baron Pearson of Rannoch, an Eton-educated peer and former Tory who took leadership of UKIP in November 2009. Pearson had already called for the UK to ban the burka, which he described as 'incompatible with Britain's values of freedom and democracy', a direct echo of Griffin's words on *Question Time*.

Above all, the EDL has been nourished by the drip-feed of anti-Muslim, anti-'political correctness' stories in Britain's press. The 'councils banning Christmas' myth, for instance, has been in constant circulation since 1998, after Birmingham City Council's marketing team decided to brand their programme of festive events 'Winterval'; this was picked up by a local newspaper and misinterpreted as an attempt to avoid offending religious sensi-tivities (it wasn't). It was then relayed by tabloids, broadsheets and even the BBC, on repeated occasions throughout the decade that followed.[31] The conversion of young, white women to Islam has been a popular topic with tabloid newspapers.

One paper, the *Daily Star*, even flirted with support for the EDL. Its sympathetic coverage culminated in a front-page story in February 2011: 'English Defence League to form political party'. Quoting a telephone poll in which 98 per cent of respon-dents allegedly professed support for the EDL's 'policies', the paper's leader column warned that 'Tommy [Robinson] and his followers will have to be taken very seriously'. Richard Peppiatt, a *Star* reporter who resigned from the paper in March 2011, explained to me how anti-Islam bias had been intensified by a desire to boost circulation:

There was a story about Muslim councillors refusing to stand up to applaud a St George's Cross winner. But they were both Respect [an anti-war party] councillors and the story didn't mention that other Muslim councillors who were present had stood up. It was presented with a picture of Tommy Robinson pointing down the camera in a very Churchillian manner and the headline was all about the EDL standing up for our soldiers, even though the EDL had nothing to do with the original story. There was a phone poll – 'do you agree with the EDL's policies?' – even though the EDL don't have any policies. A couple of thousand people phoned in, which was huge – with some polls you'd only get twenty people phoning in. So then every day we had to have a story about the EDL.[32]

Indeed, the ground on which the EDL has campaigned is so much a part of mainstream discourse that senior police officers do not appear to consider the group extremist. In April 2011, Detective Chief Superintendent Adrian Tudway, National Co-ordinator for Domestic Extremism, told a Muslim group that the EDL was 'not extreme right wing as a group, indeed if you look at their published material on their website, they are actively moving away from the right and violence with their mission statement etc.' Tudway suggested that Muslims open up a 'line of dialogue' with the EDL.[33]

In fact, the EDL's lack of a clear programme means that it has become a convenient rallying point for violent racists and fascists. Despite the group's rhetorical commitment to 'peaceful' protest, its demonstrations frequently end with Asian passers-by, or Asian-owned businesses, being attacked. In July 2011, EDL supporters picketed the family home of Sajjad Karim, a Muslim MEP who voted against the labelling of halal meat products.[34] 'EDL' has also become the rallying cry for many individual perpetrators of racist assaults, or the desecration of mosques.[35]

Rather like the National Front in its early incarnation, the

EDL is a loose coalition of different far-right currents; and just like the NF, it shows signs of being pushed in an increasingly extreme direction. Hope not Hate estimates that current and former football hooligans make up 'at least half' of any EDL protest, but several former BNP activists aside from Yaxley-Lennon have played prominent roles since the start, and members of other far-right groups including the National Front and Combat 18 have been present at demonstrations. One faction, based in the North of England and calling itself 'EDL Infidels', has broken off and is now showing a taste for more traditional fascist politics. John 'Snowy' Shaw, the Infidels' self-proclaimed leader, was quoted in June 2011 praising the anti-Semitic *Protocols of the Elders of Zion*.[36]

There are also signs that the EDL is increasingly targeting left-wing groups. In December 2010, Yaxley-Lennon threat-ened action against student anti-fees protesters; in May 2011, a group chanting 'EDL' smashed the windows of a building in Barking where a Unite Against Fascism meeting was taking place; later that year EDL supporters harassed the anti-capital-ist Occupy camps at various locations in Britain. In November, police arrested 179 EDL members near St Paul's cathedral, after repeated threats against Occupy London. Trade union build-ings and left-wing bookshops have also been targeted.[37]

The group's actions have also drawn praise from abroad, inspiring affiliates of the 'counter-jihad' network that commu-nicates through websites like Ayling's 4Freedoms. Copycat groups have sprung up around the world: on Facebook, there are groups calling themselves the Norwegian Defence League, Australian Defence League, Serbian Defence League, and many more. In March 2011, a visitor from Norway posted a message on the EDL website:

Hello. To all you good English men and women, just wanted to say that you're a blessing to all in Europe, in these dark times all of Europe are looking to you in surch [*sic*] of inspiration, courage and even hope that we might turn this evil trend with islamisation all across our continent. Well, just wanted to say keep up the good work it's good to see others that care about their country and heritage. All the best to you all Sigurd.'[38]

Four months later, 'Sigurd', whose real name was Anders Behring Breivik, murdered seventy-seven people in Oslo and at a Labour Party youth camp on the Norwegian island of Utoya. Debate continues in Norway as to whether Breivik's actions were motivated by politics or insanity, but his lengthy manifesto set out a strikingly coherent set of ideas, the bulk of which were drawn from mainstream political discourse. Eschewing neo-Nazism, professing support for Israel and opposition to the growth of Europe's Muslim population, it lashed out at the impact of 'cultural Marxism' and multiculturalism on European society. These were the coordinates for a new breed of fascism, one that mirrored the EDL's own stance.

Just as the EDL needs to proclaim non-violence in order to maintain a degree of respectability, it also needs this threatening undercurrent to keep itself in the public eye. As Ayling told the *Guardian* in March 2010, his supporters 'are not female middle-class teachers . . . if they continue to be suppressed it will turn nasty in one way or another . . . if we are going to have a mess that is so much grist to the mill.' Interviewed by the BBC after the Norway killings, he predicted similar events in Britain if people did not 'listen' to the EDL.

This lack of coherence has been the EDL's strength, but also its weakness. On the one hand, it has been possible to mobilize a wide range of supporters at short notice; on the other, these supporters often fight with one another, sapping energy from the movement. Demonstrations often result in rival football 'firms' trading blows with one another, or with the neo-Nazi elements. Yaxley-Lennon was convicted of assault in September 2011 for head-butting one of his own supporters at a rally in Blackburn.[39] Yet the EDL's instability, its innovative use of social media and its subversion of the language of human rights and anti-racism make little difference to those on the receiving end of abuse.

On 18 June 2011, twenty-nine-year-old Aftab and his younger brother Mohammed left their house in Chadwell Heath, East London, intending to rent a film from Blockbuster Video. On their way they passed a group of EDL supporters, who had gathered to protest at the construction of an Islamic centre. As the brothers waited to cross the road, protesters started chanting 'Muslim bombers off our streets'. A group broke away from the main EDL protest and attacked the pair, knocking Mohammed to the ground and kicking him while he was down. One EDL steward accused his fellow demonstrators of 'behaving like fucking animals',[40] but did not intervene. Mohammed was left needing hospital treatment.

Aftab had grown up in a very different London from that of his parents, who moved from Pakistan in the 1970s and had experienced racist abuse in their youth. 'Chadwell Heath always felt like a safe place,' he told me. 'But [the attack] has really shattered my perception of the area.'

By a small coincidence, the attack took place only a mile or so from where Syeda Choudhury, the British Bengali whose teenage experiences of the Isle of Dogs were recounted in Chapter One, now lived. Following the trajectory of many East

Londoners, white, black and Asian, she had moved out to the suburbs; her son, a baby at the time of Derek Beackon's election, was grown up, and she now had a young teenage daughter. I interviewed Choudhury not long after the attack on Aftab and Mohammed, and she told me how her daughter had recently come running home from school in hysterics, because a rumour had gone round that the EDL were on the prowl. 'It's changed so much from where we were [in 1993],' Choudhury said. 'But that just made me think, oh my god, are we going back to the old days?'

In the aftermath of the Norway attacks, as the media's gaze fell once more on right-wing extremism, one figure was absent from mainstream media outlets: Nick Griffin. His verdict, delivered to followers of his Twitter feed, was that Breivik was 'not a nationalist but a free market liberal, anti-Muslim Zionist' influenced by a 'neo-con Clash of Civilisations [and] civic nationalism' rather than 'our ideology'. In his view Breivik was 'as likely to be part of [a] Strategy of Tension by our Masters than [a] genuine reaction to Islamic threat'. Clinging to his biological racism and conspiracy theories, Griffin now looked as out-dated among the far right as John Tyndall once had.

Three days after the attacks, Griffin was narrowly re-elected leader of the BNP. After the 2010 election the party had slid back into irrelevance, losing scores more council seats the following year. His challenger was Andrew Brons, whose campaign highlighted chaotic party finances and the recent electoral disasters, which were blamed squarely on Griffin's *Question Time* performance.[41] But the fact that Brons, an ageing neo-Nazi, was the best candidate Griffin's critics could muster showed just how depleted the party had become. Griffin scraped the election by seven votes (1,157 to 1,148), but fewer than 3,000 members had bothered to vote at all. At its peak, the BNP had claimed well over 10,000.

In August 2011, after riots and looting broke out in English cities – with EDL members reportedly on hand to 'defend' largely white areas of outer London such as Enfield and Eltham, Griffin complained to supporters that his perspective had been completely ignored by the BBC.[42] In contrast with the riots that had erupted in England's North a decade previously, this time nobody was listening to him.

Yet the BNP's main line of propaganda – that Britain was being undermined from within by racial mixing and an undeserving poor – was willingly repeated by the celebrity historian David Starkey, live on *Newsnight*. 'A substantial section of the chavs have become black,' he bemoaned. 'The whites have become black . . . Black and white, boy and girl operate in this language together. This language which is wholly false, which is a Jamaican patois, that's been intruded [*sic*] in England and this is why so many of us have this sense of literally a foreign country.'

Nick Griffin may have gone, but to what extent do the old fears remain?

Conclusion

Ten Myths about Britain's Far Right

The threat has passed

To be clear: Nick Griffin's project has failed. The BNP never shook off its associations with neo-Nazism and violence, and thanks in part to one of the largest anti-fascist mobilizations this country has ever seen, its support did not spread very far beyond a hard core of voters. The English Defence League has also been pushed back by counter-demonstrations, and its attempts to build a political wing by linking up with another BNP splinter group, British Freedom, have so far been unsuccessful. Yet although the BNP was severely damaged as an organization, and its morale was smashed at the 2010 general election, the fact remains that its vote held up, indicating a small but apparently solid base of support.

Anti-immigration sentiment remains among the population at large, and discontent with mainstream politics is growing, as indicated by record low turnouts at parliamentary by-elections in 2012. UKIP has been the main beneficiary of this discontent. In by-elections such as the one in Rotherham on 29 November 2012, it has pitched for the BNP vote. Its leadership is careful not to say anything overtly racist, but the party focuses its attacks on 'multiculturalism' and boasts policies such as a pledge to deny immigrants access to the welfare state.

Meanwhile, Griffin, along with the BNP's Andrew Brons, remains an MEP. The BNP has splintered, with activists forming several different smaller parties, each one of which is vying to establish itself as the new force on the far right. Some diehard neo-Nazis have rejoined the National Front, while others have followed Brons into a new grouping, the British Democratic Party. Those activists more interested in winning elections, led by Eddy Butler, joined the English Democrats, a right-wing, anti-immigration party whose candidate was elected mayor of Doncaster in 2009.

As a movement, the far right is in disarray, which increases the likelihood of 'lone wolf' violent attacks by frustrated individuals, like the 1999 London nail bombings or Breivik's massacre in Norway in 2011. And mainstream politicians will continue to invoke the presence of the far right to justify their own policies.

The rise of the BNP was a consequence of 'too much' immigration

Without a doubt, 'immigration' was the main reason voters chose the BNP. But it relied on the hugely distorted public perception of immigrants, created largely by inaccurate press coverage. A survey carried out by Oxford University's Migration Observatory in the autumn of 2011, for instance, found that members of the public were most likely to associate immigration with asylum-seekers, or illegal immigrants, even though these only make up a tiny proportion of the total.[1]

There's a further problem, too: when a BNP supporter expresses an opposition to 'immigration', are they referring to people who have newly arrived in the country? Or do they regard non-white Britons as 'immigrants', even though they may have been born in this country? As John Cave, a BNP activist from Burnley, told me, the reason the BNP existed was 'to give people a chance to say they don't want multiculturalism, they don't want integration and they want, as Mr Tyndall used to say, a white Britain'. The BNP did well in some areas that were experiencing new immigration, such as Barking and Dagenham, but also in towns with settled non-white populations, such as Burnley or Stoke-on-Trent.

Racism only played a minor role in driving BNP support

'I don't suggest that everyone who votes BNP is racist,' said the Conservative shadow minister for communities Eric Pickles in 2009, the day after Nick Griffin and Andrew Brons were elected to the European Parliament. 'If we do that, the BNP benefits.'

In one sense, Pickles was right: blanket condemnation of BNP voters by mainstream politicians would have been a strategic mistake. For peripheral supporters, tempted to vote for the BNP because of their dismay at a lack of housing, or a feeling of being ignored by the three big parties, this would merely have confirmed their suspicion that politics was run by an uncaring elite.

But the best available information on the attitudes of BNP voters speaks for itself. A significant proportion shared the BNP's biological racism – that black people, for instance, were intellectually inferior to whites. A greater number still held strongly hostile attitudes to Islam. The immigrants who most exercised BNP voters, and whom the BNP targeted most often with its propaganda, were non-white.

This took place against a background where the flames of

popular racism were fanned by the press. In the past decade, asylum-seekers and Muslims have been described in terms that nobody today would ever dare use for Jews, or even Afro-Caribbeans. The argument that anti-Muslim prejudice is less of a problem since it's directed at religion rather than skin colour, holds little weight: ever since Enoch Powell, the fear of alien cultures has been a central feature of racist discourse. Today, the 'cultural' fear of Islam marshalled by the EDL slips easily into racist violence directed at 'Pakis'.

The point is that the BNP gained support by exploiting racism *in combination with* economic resentment. It targeted people who felt like they had been passed over for housing, or for regeneration money, but who also resented the presence of 'Africans' in their borough, or felt that it was unfair for Asians to be given resources, even when they were demonstrably in greater need. When the BNP was defeated, it was by campaigners who offered voters a positive, non-racist alternative. 'I'm not racist, but I don't think these Asians should get houses before us whites,' is a racist statement – but kick away the economic grievance which underpins it, and you undermine the racism on which parties like the BNP thrive.

White people in Britain are discriminated against because of their skin colour

In January 2012, the evening after two of Stephen Lawrence's killers were finally convicted of murder, the black Labour MP Diane Abbott made an ill-advised comment on Twitter, in which she suggested that white people 'love playing "divide and rule" We should not play their game #tacticasoldascolonialism.' Soul-searching over the

Lawrence case was put on hold as a range of right-wing commentators rushed to condemn Abbott for her 'racism'.

Surely this was proof – just as the BNP argued – that racism 'cuts both ways'? Well, no. As one defender of Abbott neatly put it, 'I can imagine a world in which Diane Abbott's tweet . . . would be racist. In this parallel universe Britain is dominated, politically and economically, by an unshakeable clique of black, working-class women and two black men have just been convicted, several years too late, thanks to an institutionally racist black police force, of the murder of white teenager Stephen Lawrence.'[2]

In twenty-first-century England and Wales, you are thirty times more likely to be stopped and searched by police if you are black.[3] Black and Asian people in Britain remain at a statistical disadvantage in employment opportunities and access to housing. Anti-racism laws are intended to level the playing field. Complaining about 'anti-white' discrimination, as the BNP has done, is in fact an attempt to preserve privilege rather than remove it. There are indeed ways in which some white people in Britain are unfairly held back, but these have nothing to do with their skin colour.

'Tough talk' keeps the far right at bay

In the early 90s, when the Lib Dems in Tower Hamlets offered housing for 'Sons and Daughters', it opened the way for the BNP to win a seat in Millwall. In 2000, when William Hague made immigration a national election issue for the first time since 1979, it did nothing to halt the early growth of the BNP. In 2002, when David Blunkett accused asylum seekers of 'swamping' British schools, it did not stop the BNP making its breakthrough in

Burnley. And when the Labour Government then decided to 'triangulate' BNP voters, the problem spread. In 2006, after Margaret Hodge claimed her constituents couldn't get homes for their children because of immigration, the BNP won eleven seats on Barking and Dagenham council. In 2009, when Gordon Brown promised 'British Jobs for British Workers', workers threw the slogan back in his face, and the BNP went on to win two seats in the European Parliament. The latest politician to join in is the current prime minister, David Cameron. In April 2011, he suggested that 'immigration and welfare reform are two sides of the same coin . . . we will never control immigration properly unless we tackle welfare dependency.'

Blaming immigrants for the failings of the welfare state only fuels the misperceptions that drive support for the far right. If people complain they can't get council houses, for instance, then the only honest question a politician can ask is 'why aren't there more council houses?' If there are large numbers of people receiving unemployment benefit or tax credits, then the only honest question is 'why is the economy failing to provide more jobs, or pay sustainable wages?'

Anti-racism has been imposed on the white working class by a politically-correct elite

'I used to hate working there,' Jim Brinklow told me, as we sat in his car at what was once the entrance to Ford's paint, trim and assembly plant in Dagenham. 'But it breaks my heart to see it gone.' During the 1980s, Brinklow, a white East Londoner, worked on the assembly line at Ford, where he was a convenor for his trade union branch. While Dagenham, where most Ford workers lived, was a largely white area, many black and Asian workers, from elsewhere in East London, also had jobs at the factory. Most of them worked alongside Jim on the assembly line – regarded as the worst job at Ford's – and found that they were blocked from taking better-paid jobs elsewhere on the site. 'When I started at the plant,' said Jim, 'there was a lot of nastiness. Lots of racist graffiti on the toilet walls.' The far right was also active: during the 1980s, the BNP member Tony Lecomber – the convicted bomber who would later become Griffin's head of 'group development' – was employed as a foreman at the plant.

Brinklow and his fellow workers took a stand. 'Two foremen were distributing a racist leaflet. So we went on strike, we stopped the production line. We said to the company something's radically wrong here when you have two foremen distributing stuff like that. As a result Ford set up an equal opportunities committee. We insisted on monthly meetings. They began advertising jobs in the local press, the black press. They set up a prayer room for Muslims. Then black Christians began to complain "what about us, we want a prayer room". They got one.'

This is what anti-racism looks like. 'Equal opportunities' are not handed down from on high by Westminster bureaucrats; they have been fought for by ordinary men and women. Even at its peak, the BNP never spoke for anywhere near the majority of working-class whites – in Dagenham, or anywhere else.

The growth of the BNP and the emergence of the EDL indicate the failure of multiculturalism

Readers may be tempted to see the BNP as evidence that Britain really is becoming a nation of ethnic and cultural ghettos, where there are 'no-go zones' for non-Muslims and that communities are living increasingly 'parallel lives'. In fact, as the 2011 census results indicate, the trend is moving in the opposite direction: ethnic minorities are spreading more evenly across Britain.[4] What's more, areas of cities with concentrated ethnic minority populations tend not to be 'ghettos': think of Burnley, where even the 'Asian' areas of Daneshouse and Stoneyholme are still around 40 per cent white.

Yet the idea that Britain is a nation divided by race and culture, rather than wealth, persists across a wide range of right-wing and liberal opinion, with 'multiculturalism' being named the culprit. Beneath these anxieties, however, exists the everyday, thriving multiculturalism of modern Britain; the result of our daily inter-actions with one another. Each one of us is unique, yet each one of us has habits and customs and ways of seeing the world that overlap. Culture is not a fixed set of attributes, nor is it handed down by decree; it's what we do. This is a fact that even the BNP was forced to accept. That's why Griffin had to set up an 'ethnic liaison committee', and it's why, in the end he had to tell his party to 'adapt or die' and accept non-white members. The EDL is further evidence of how the far right has had to accommodate to the reality of modern Britain.

The BNP was Labour's problem alone

The BNP saw its greatest successes in what were once Labour strongholds. Barking and Dagenham, Burnley, Stoke-on-Trent, even Tower Hamlets – these were all boroughs that had been solidly Labour for decades. Yet analysis of the BNP vote suggests that supporters were only marginally more likely to have come from Labour-voting backgrounds. What the BNP benefited from was a much larger fall in Labour support: in Barking, for instance, Margaret Hodge's vote plummeted from well over 21,000 in 1997, to under 14,000 in 2005. By contrast, in 2005 the BNP could only attract 4,900 votes.

Yet when one mainstream party suffers a drop in support, another usually steps in to fill the gap. Where, we might ask, were the Tories? Where were the Lib Dems? Why did BNP voters feel that all three main parties had nothing to offer them – and why, more broadly, did an official commission conclude in 2006 that there was a 'well-ingrained popular view across the country that our political institutions and their politicians are failing, untrustworthy, and disconnected from the great mass of the British people'?

The BNP wasn't fascist

As the BNP's own Language and Concepts Discipline Manual advised, Nick Griffin wished his party to be perceived as a 'right-wing populist party' that espoused 'right-of-centre views traditional to ordinary working people who are not leftists'. In fact, throughout its existence, the BNP has remained profoundly fascist, dedicated to a 'revolution' that would make Britain an ethnically 'pure' society. The BNP had its roots in the most extreme sections of Britain's far right. Griffin developed his own personal ideology from a concoction of 'left-wing' Nazism, racist mysticism and ideas borrowed from the French Front National about how to pursue 'cultural hegemony' in order to win political power. After taking over the BNP, he attempted to fashion a respectable public image behind which these ideas could be hidden. Yet even as the BNP tried to distance itself in public from violence, it still attracted supporters who harboured fantasies about armed conflict. In 2006, a former BNP member Robert Cottage was jailed for stockpiling explosive chemicals at his Lancashire home. Another ex-member, Terence Gavan, was jailed in 2010 for hoarding guns and home-made bombs in his bedroom. A rise in reported hate crime followed the election of BNP councillors in the West Midlands, London and Essex.[5]

What's more, while the BNP attracted a layer of working-class support, it kept some roots in the middle classes, the traditional bedrock of fascism. Griffin was the privately educated son of a businessman; party members included company directors, computing entrepreneurs, bankers and estate agents. The genesis of the English Defence League indicates similar foundations. It has enjoyed the perception, reflected across the national media, of being a spontaneous expression of working-class anger, sprung directly from the street. The origin of this group, which was conceived of in a £500,000 apartment, and shaped by a group of anti-Muslim ideologues including a director of a City investment fund and a property developer, suggest a more complex picture. The EDL has displayed increasingly fascist-like behaviour, targeting not only Muslims but left-wing movements too.

'It couldn't happen here'

The communities among which the BNP thrived were those whose inhabitants had reasons to feel pessimistic, even during the boom years. Its voters were often skilled workers who had done well for themselves, but felt their position threatened. Now, during the worst economic crisis in a century, with a coalition government whose austerity policies are guaranteed to spread despondency further still, people have more reason than ever to worry about the future.

Across Europe, the financial crisis has inflamed tensions between a global market, a multinational EU and nation states that still count on patriotism as a social glue. Right-wing populism of various hues is on the rise, with neo-fascists in France and Hungary making electoral gains; the continued success of anti-Muslim parties in Holland, Belgium and elsewhere; and 'nativist' movements such as Finland's True Finns causing electoral upsets for the more established political parties. Crisis in the eurozone has led to the emergence of Greece's Golden Dawn, an unashamedly neo-Nazi movement that swept into parliament at the country's general election of May 2012. And the conspiracy theories cited by Anders Behring Breivik – that 'cultural Marxists' are in charge of public institutions like the BBC and that Europe is threatened by a Muslim takeover – have currency within mainstream political discourse.

In Britain, all three main parties are committed to varying degrees of austerity. We had a taste of the anger that can arise at feeling locked out of the political system when students smashed the windows of the Treasury in 2010. Perhaps aware of this, the coalition has been pursuing a media strategy that seeks to shift public anger onto convenient scapegoats: the unemployed, people on disability benefits and immigrants – who have been blamed at one and the same time for being benefit scroungers and for taking 'British' jobs. In December 2012, for instance, the Tory Home Secretary Theresa May told the *Daily Telegraph* that immigrants were responsible for rising house prices, unemployment and low wages.

Societies that promise equality, freedom and democracy, yet

preside over massive inequalities of wealth, are breeding grounds for racism and other vicious resentments. And wherever these resentments exist, the far right will try to exploit them. The fascism of the 1920s and 1930s succeeded because it played on wider fears, winning the support of those who would never have thought of themselves as 'extremists'. The Nazis used anti-Semitism because it already existed in German society. Their successors today use Islamophobia and the hatred of migrants because it already exists in our societies. We do not need to wait for a successor to the BNP to emerge before addressing these much deeper problems.

It's September 2011, and I'm sitting with a group of activists from Unite Against Fascism in the garden of the Half Moon pub near Stepney Green in East London. It's the early evening, and I've been tagging along on their counter-demonstration against the English Defence League. In an echo of Mosley's Blackshirts, more than seventy years previously, the far right were trying to march through a cosmopolitan area of the East End, hoping to stir up conflict. This time, the EDL had targeted the East London mosque in Whitechapel and the UAF activists were jubilant at having prevented them by blocking the road, joined by several thousand local residents.

Our conversation is drowned out by the sound of a police helicopter flying low. There's a commotion further down the road, and the pub bouncers slam shut the iron gates that lead on to the street. We poke our head through the bars and try to see what's happening. It's a coachload of EDL supporters, someone says. Then the coach drives past. One of the large windows on the side is completely smashed. There's a smell of burning rubber. Hundreds of Bengali youths are running alongside the coach. 'Come to *my* area?' I can hear one saying indignantly as he charges up the street? Police in riot gear are legging it up the road trying to overtake the Bengalis. One police officer, who has caught up, is trying to slow down the youths. 'They're cunts, but just leave it, yeah?' The EDL members are looking out and jeering; as they pass the pub, patrons stick their hands through the gates and give them the finger. A white cockney woman shouts 'go on, fuck off'. She turns to me and says: 'I hope they get everything they deserve. Bloody racists. How dare they come here?'

I turn round and see my companions locked in debate with a family on the neighbouring table. It looks less friendly. I'm just trying to catch what's being said when a woman in her forties stands up and shouts: 'I'm a Huguenot, my family were immigrants, but these Pakis don't work for a living.' She accuses one of the activists: 'You've got no idea what it's like here. Where are you from?' 'Manchester,' is the reply. 'Well why don't you fuck off back to Manchester then!'

Another UAF activist is embroiled in a discussion with a young white man of about twenty. 'They [the EDL] are doing it in the wrong way but what they're saying is right,' the young man insists. He is complaining that the Bengalis don't work and they all get to the front of the housing queue. 'They get away with anything. How is it there's all these protests about EDL, but when Muslims turn up and burn poppies at a funeral for dead soldiers nobody says anything?' The UAF activist, a working-class Northerner, is trying to explain that there's no point people having a go at one another because of their skin colour or religion when the real division is between rich and poor. The young man replies, 'fair enough, but nobody was talking about any of this stuff before they started.' I chip in: aren't we supposed to have political parties that can talk about this without it leading to a riot.

'Yeah, so what does that tell you about *them*?' he says.

Acknowledgements

I'm grateful to all my interviewees for their time and for their openness – without their cooperation this book would not have been possible.

There are also a large number of people whose conversations, contacts, and generally wise advice have been essential. They are: Anthony Barnett, Jamie Bartlett, Rita Bensley, Anindya Bhattacharyya, John Biggs, David Braniff-Herbert, Jim Brinklow, Robin Burrett, Joel Busher, Joe Caluori, Brian Cathcart, Valeria Costa-Kostritsky, Jon Cruddas, John Eden, Matthew Goodwin, Wendy Graham, Olwen Hamer, Gareth Harris, Sophie Heawood, Nicholas Holtam, Sarah Honeysett, Eve Hostettler, Sunny Hundal, Miranda Iossifidis, Arun Kundnani, Peter Lazenby, Anna Livingstone, James Macintyre, Melanie McFadyean, Cas Mudde, Peter Oborne, Bhikhu Parekh, James Rhodes, Darren Rodwell, Ruth Rosenau, Sukran Sahin, Paul Sillett, Sam Tarry, Matthew Taunton, Mike Waite, Georgie Wemyss, Jim Wolfreys, Gary Younge, my family and all my colleagues at the *New Statesman*.

Special thanks are reserved for Nigel Fountain, Ryan Gilbey, Zakia Uddin and Vron Ware, for their perceptive and helpful comments on the manuscript, and for my editors at Verso: Tom Penn, who got me started, and Leo Hollis, who got me finished.

This book was enabled by a grant from the Authors' Foundation.

Notes

Chapter 1. A Nasty Local Difficulty

1 Georgie Wemyss, *The Invisible Empire: White Discourse, Tolerance and Belonging*, London: Ashgate, 2009, p. 127.

2 Janet Foster, *Docklands: Cultures in Conflict, Worlds in Collision*, London: UCL, 1999, p. 39.

3 Ibid., pp. 148–9; Interview with Rita Bensley, Association of Island Communities, 20 June 2011.

4 Docklands Forum, 'Race and Housing in London's Docklands', January 1993.

5 Ibid.

6 *East London Advertiser*, 23 September 1993.

7 Docklands Forum, 'Race and Housing in London's Docklands'.

8 The '18' refers to the first and eighth letters of the alphabet, Adolf Hitler's initials.

9 Photo published in *Searchlight*, July 2010.

10 A full account of this period can be found in Matthew Collins, *Hate: My Life in the British Far Right*, London: Biteback, 2011.

11 In 1991, after a black teenager, Rolan Adams, was stabbed to death on the Thamesmead estate in south-east London, the BNP organized a march along the road where he died. Adams's parents received racist phone calls and every other house on their street was leafleted with extremist material. The next year,

an Asian teenager, Rohit Duggal, was stabbed to death in Eltham. After Stephen Lawrence's murder, anti-fascists pointed to a surge in racist attacks since the BNP had set up shop in Welling in 1990.

12 Eddy Butler, 'How We Won Millwall', *Patriot*, issue 1, 1997.

13 Ibid.

14 An account of militant anti-fascism during the 1980s and 1990s can be found in Sean Birchall, *Beating the Fascists: the Untold Story of Anti-Fascist Action*, London: Freedom Press, 2011.

15 Docklands Forum, 'Race and Housing in London's Docklands'.

16 Ibid.

17 Butler, 'How We Won Millwall'.

18 'Political Speech and Race Relations in a Liberal Democracy, Report of an Inquiry into the Conduct of the Tower Hamlets Liberal Democrats in Publishing Allegedly Racist Election Literature between 1990 and 1993', December 1993.

19 *East London Advertiser*, 23 September 1993.

20 *East London Advertiser*, 9 September 1993. The Liberal Democrats dismissed Labour's canvass return as 'fiction'.

21 *East London Advertiser*, 23 September 1993.

22 Nicholas Holtam and Sue Mayo, 'Learning from the Conflict: Reflections on the Struggle Against the British National Party on the Isle of Dogs, 1993–4', London: Jubilee Group, 1998.

23 *Daily Mail*, 20 September 1993.

24 *News of the World*, 26 September 1993.

25 *East London Advertiser*, 21 April 1994; *Independent*, 18 June 1994.

26 Foster, *Docklands*, p. 270.

27 Ibid., p. 266.

28 *East London Advertiser*, 23 December 1993.

29 *Socialist Review*, June 1994.

30 Interview with Nicholas Holtam, 3 February 2011.

31 Holtam and Mayo, 'Learning from the Conflict'.

32 Interview with the author, 20 June 2011.

33 *East London Advertiser*, 3 March 1994.

34 Wemyss, *Invisible Empire*, pp. 95–119.

35 *East London Advertiser*, 24 March 1994.

36 *East London Advertiser*, 5 May 1994.

37 Butler, 'How We Won Millwall'.

Chapter 2. Any Colour as Long as It's Black

1 Quote from *The Rune* in Roger Eatwell and Cas Mudde, *Western Democracies and the New Extreme Right Challenge*, London: Routledge, 2004.

2 Paul Foot, *The Rise of Enoch Powell: An Examination of Enoch Powell's Attitude to Immigration and Race*, London: Cornmarket, 1969, p. 136.

3 John Bean, *Many Shades of Black: Inside Britain's Far Right*, UK: Hedgerow, 1999, p. 206.

4 Foot, *The Rise of Enoch Powell*, p. 126.

5 Martin Walker, *The National Front*, London: Fontana, 1977, p. 145.

6 Stan Taylor, *The National Front in English Politics*, London: Macmillan, 1982, p. 111.

7 Martin Barker, *The New Racism: Conservatives and the Ideology of the Tribe*, London: Junction, 1991, p. 20.

8 *Nationalism Today*, issue 7.

9 If any of this sounds familiar to David Cameron's 'Big Society' rhetoric, it's no accident: Phillip Blond, guru of the Big Society, draws heavily on Distributism in his book *Red Tory*, London: Faber and Faber, 2010.

10 The *Sturmabteilung*, or SA, was the first Nazi paramilitary group. Gregor Strasser was a regional leader.

11 *Nationalism Today*, issue 11.

12 Roger Eatwell, 'The Esoteric Ideology of the National Front in the 1980s', in Mike Cronin, ed., *The Failure of British Fascism:*

The Far-Right and the Fight for Political Recognition, London: Palgrave Macmillan, 1996, pp. 108–9.

13 Peter Fysh and Jim Wolfreys, *The Politics of Racism in France*, London: Palgrave Macmillan, 2003, p. 100.

14 Ray Hill, *The Other Face of Terror: Inside Europe's Neo-Nazi Network*, London: Grafton, 1988, pp. 192–3.

15 Derek Holland, 'The Political Soldier: A Statement', 1984.

16 *National Front News*, issue 93, 1987; Eatwell, 'Esoteric Ideology' in *The Failure of British Fascism*, pp. 108–9.

17 *Nationalism Today*, issue 41.

18 *From Ballots to Bombs: The Inside Story of the National Front's Political Soldiers*, London: Searchlight Publishing, 1989 (authors uncredited).

19 Private information.

Chapter 3. The Führer of Notting Hill

1 George Thayer, *The British Political Fringe*, London: Anthony Blond, 1965, pp. 13–32.

2 Tyndall's early years are recounted in his autobiography, *Eleventh Hour: Call for British Rebirth*, Albion Press, 1988.

3 Named after the Conservative Chancellor Rab Butler and his Labour counterpart Hugh Gaitskell.

4 Bean, *Many Shades of Black*, p. 126.

5 Ibid., p. 127.

6 Walker, *The National Front*, p. 35.

7 Bean, *Many Shades of Black*, p. 143.

8 Ibid., p. 146.

9 Thayer, *The British Political Fringe*, p. 19.

10 Tyndall, *Eleventh Hour*, p. 183.

11 Richard Thurlow, *Fascism in Britain: From Oswald Mosley's Blackshirts to the National Front*, London: IB Tauris, 1998, p. 237.

12 Walker, *The National Front*, p. 46.

13 Foot, *The Rise of Enoch Powell*, p. 168.

14 Walker, *The National Front*, pp. 51–67.

15 Hill, *The Other Face of Terror*, p. 166.

16 Ibid., pp. 148–9.

17 Since the 1980s, Bercow has softened his right-wing stance and is today regarded as one of the most socially liberal Conservative MPs.

18 On this occasion, the BNP did not bite. The journalist who wrote the *Guardian* story later apologized to Staines for any suggestion that he held racist or fascist views.

19 *Guardian*, 31 May 1986; 5 July 1986.

20 *Guardian*, 17 July 1986.

21 *Guardian*, 6 September 1985.

Chapter 4. Forget about the Ideas and Think about Selling Them

1   Interview with Eddy Butler, 21 January 2011.

2   *Guardian*, 15 November 1991.

3   *Observer*, 16 June 1991.

4   See Early Day Motion 382, 11 December 1991, www.partiament. uk/edm/1991-92/382.

5   Interview with Nick Griffin, 24 February 2011.

6   Nick Lowles, *White Riot: The Rise and Fall of Combat 18*, London: Milo, 2001, pp. 14–17.

7   Ibid., p. 142.

8   *Spearhead*, issue 334, December 1996, p. 13.

9   Nigel Copsey, *Contemporary British Fascism: The British National Party and the Quest for Legitimacy*, London: Palgrave Macmillan, 2005, p. 70.

10 Ibid., p. 72.

11 Interview with Nick Griffin, 24 February 2011.

12 Fysh and Wolfreys, *The Politics of Racism in France*, p. 140.

13 *Spearhead*, issue 351, May 1998.

14 A concept outlined by Fysh and Wolfreys in *The Politics of Racism in France*.

15 *Spearhead*, issue 348, February 1997.

16 *Spearhead*, issue 352, May 1998.

17 *Spearhead*, issue 351, April 1998.

18 *Spearhead*, issue 352, May 1998.

19 *Spearhead*, issue 351, April 1998.

20 Les Back and Vron Ware, *Out of Whiteness: Color, Politics and Culture*, University of Chicago Press, 2002, p. 49.

21 *Spearhead*, issue 352, April 1998.

22 *Spearhead*, issue 361, March 1999.

23 *Spearhead*, issue 357, November 1998.

24 *Spearhead*, issue 354, August 1998.

25 *Spearhead*, issue 366, August 1999.

26 Copsey, *Contemporary British Fascism*, pp. 104–6.

27 *Spearhead*, issue 366, August 1999.

28 Copsey, *Contemporary British Fascism*, p. 110.

29 *Spearhead*, issue 367, September 1999.

30 Copsey, *Contemporary British Fascism*, p. 100.

31 *Spearhead*, issue 368, October 1998.

32 Interview with Nick Griffin, 24 February 2011.

Chapter 5. The Most Tolerant Race on Earth

1 It was not entirely unusual for women to take influential positions in far-right politics. Indeed, the British Fascisti, the first group in this country to imitate Mussolini, was founded in 1923 by Rotha Lintorn-Orman, who had served in the Women's Reserve Ambulance during the First World War and was a staunch anti-Communist. Aside from Francoise Dior, the aristocrats Lady Jane Birdwood and Rosine de Bounevialle had been prominent far-right activists in the post-war period. But the BNP under John Tyndall's

leadership had featured no women in senior roles, or as prominent election candidates.

2 http://www.freedompartyuk.net/public/articles/sharron. html; originally published in *Spearhead*.

3 Copsey, *Contemporary British Fascism*, p. 113.

4 As Griffin told an audience of far-right activists in the US in April 2000, the BNP 'isn't about selling out its ideas, which are your ideas too, but we are determined to sell them. And that means basically to use saleable words – freedom, security, identity, democracy . . . So instead of talking about racial purity, we talk about identity.' The seminar, where Griffin met with American white supremacists including the former Ku Klux Klan Grand Wizard David Duke, was organized through American Friends of the BNP, which raised funds for the party until it closed in 2001.

5 Francis Wheen, 'The right revs up', *Guardian*, 13 October 1999, guardian.co.uk.

6 http://web.archive.org/web/20010304020342/http://bnp. org.uk/library/raceact.html.

7 Mark Deavin, with whose help Griffin had sketched out the 'four concepts' to BNP members in the late 90s, did not take up a formal role in the revamped party.

8 *Identity*, January 2001 issue.

9 *Identity*, March 2001 issue; http://web.archive.org/web/20011026050735/http://bnp.org.uk/article11.html.

10 http://web.archive.org/web/20010304015651/http://bnp. org.uk/library/revoltn.html; originally published in 1998, this article was still posted on the BNP website as late as February 2002, titled 'We're living in interesting times!' and credited to 'Chairman Nick Griffin'.

11 Ibid.

12 Gary Younge, 'The Death of Stephen Lawrence: The Macpherson Report', *The Political Quarterly*, vol. 70, no.3 (July 1999), pp. 329–334

13 Tony Blair's speech to the Labour Party conference, September 1999.

14 Brian Cathcart, *The Case of Stephen Lawrence*, London: Penguin, 2000, p. 355.

15 *The Sun*, 2 March 1999.

16 http://news.bbc.co.uk/hi/english/static/special_report/1999/11/99/battle_for_london/candidates/m_newland.stm.

17 Chris Mullin, *A View from the Foothills*, London: Profile, 2010.

18 Arun Kundnani, *The End of Tolerance: Racism in 21ˢᵗ Century Britain*, London: Pluto, 2007, p. 66.

19 *Campaign Against Racism and Fascism*, issue 48, February–March 1999.

20 Ibid.

21 *Daily Mirror*, 13 March 2000.

22 Jack Straw declined to be interviewed for this book.

23 'Britain Today – Are We an Intolerant Nation?' *Reader's Digest*, October 2000, ipsos-mori.com.

24 http://web.archive.org/web/20010611211812/http://bnp.org.uk/resources/asylum.pdf.

25 *Campaign Against Racism and Fascism*, issue 56, June–July 2000.

26 Ibid.

27 Copsey, *Contemporary British Fascism*, p. 115.

28 Paul Kelso, 'The suburb where one in four voted BNP', *Guardian*, 15 July 2000, guardian.co.uk.

29 Tony Blair, *A Journey*, London: Hutchinson, 2010, pp. 523–4.

30 Kevin Toolis, 'Race to the right', *Guardian*, 20 May 2000, guardian.co.uk.

31 *Spearhead*, issue 366, August 1999; Dispatches: *Young, Nazi and Proud*, Channel 4, 2002.

32 *Searchlight*, September 2000.

33 Ibid.

34 *Searchlight*, November 2000.

35 True Stories: *The Battle for Barking*, Channel 4, 2010.

36 http://www.spearhead.com/0110-jt1.html.
37 The Parekh Report, *The Future of Multi-Ethnic Britain*, Profile Books, 2000.
38 http://news.bbc.co.uk/1/hi/uk/966629.stm.
39 Blair, *A Journey*, p. 90.

Chapter 6. One Law for Them and Another for Us

1 The account of rioting in Burnley is taken from 'Burnley Speaks, Who Listens? Report of the Burnley Task Force – Summary of the Clarke Report', Burnley Council, June 2001.
2 *Spearhead*, various issues, 1998.
3 Paul Bagguley and Yasmin Hussain, *Riotous Citizens: Ethnic Conflict in Multicultural Britain*, London: Ashgate, 2008, p. 46.
4 Lowles, *White Riot*, p. xi.
5 Jeevan Vasagar, 'Far right aims to gain foothold in Oldham', *Guardian*, 30 May 2001.
6 *The Times*, 9 June 2001.
7 Football hooliganism has historically been fertile recruiting territory for far-right movements.
8 Private information.
9 Figures supplied by Burnley Borough Council.
10 James Rhodes, 'The Political Breakthrough of the BNP: The Case of Burnley', *British Politics*, vol. 4, no. 1 (April 2009).
11 Ibid.
12 Steven Smith, *How it was Done: The Rise of Burnley BNP*, Burnley: Cliviger Press, 2004, p. 70.
13 'Burnley Speaks, Who Listens? Report of the Burnley Task Force'.
14 http://news.bbc.co.uk/1/hi/uk/1436867.stm.
15 Blair, *A Journey*, pp. 523–4.
16 Panorama: *The Secret Agent*, BBC, July 2004.
17 Gary Younge, 'The boundaries of race in Britain', *Guardian*, 25 April 2005.

18 Private information.

19 Smith, *How it was Done*, p. 53.

20 'BNP: the Roots of its Appeal', Democratic Audit, 2006.

21 Nigel Copsey, 'The Labour Party's Response to the National Front and British National Party', in Nigel Copsey and David Renton, eds, *British Fascism, the Labour Movement and the State*, London: Palgrave Macmillan, 2005, p. 190.

22 A full account of this process can be found in Jonathan Marcus, *The National Front and French Politics*, London: Palgrave Macmillan, 1995.

23 Copsey and Renton, *British Fascism*, p. 191.

24 David Blunkett, *The Blunkett Tapes: My Life in the Bear Pit*, London: Bloomsbury, 2006, pp. 601–2.

25 Diary entry for 23 January 2003 in Mullin, *A View from the Foothills*.

26 Peter Oborne, *The Triumph of the Political Class*, London: Pocket Books, 2006, p. 248.

27 Blunkett, *The Blunkett Tapes*, p. 491.

28 *Burnley Express*, 7 May 2002.

29 James Rhodes, '"It's Not Just Them, it's Whites as Well": Whiteness, Class and BNP support', *Sociology*, vol. 45, no. 1 (February 2011), pp. 102–117.

30 Paul Harris, 'Mythical refugees help BNP win white suburb', *Guardian*, 11 May 2003; interview with Eddy Butler, 24 January 2011.

31 Information supplied by Peter Lazenby, Yorkshire-based journalist and anti-fascist campaigner.

32 Interview with Steven Smith, 5 July 2011.

33 Panorama: *The Secret Agent*.

34 *Lancashire Evening Telegraph*, 6 May 2003.

35 Private information.

36 Kevin Ovenden, '"Why I have left the BNP" – Burnley councillor', *Socialist Worker*, issue 1891, 6 March, 2004; Tash Shifrin, 'Dazed and confused', *Guardian*, 24 March 2004.

Chapter 7. We're the Labour Party Your Parents Voted for

1 General Secretary of the RMT.

2 Although Becontree is regarded as part of Dagenham, it falls mostly within the constituency boundary of Barking. I refer to it as 'Dagenham' throughout this chapter, since that's the way people who live there refer to it.

3 'Power to the People: The Report of Power, an Independent Inquiry into Britain's Democracy', Joseph Rowntree Reform Trust, 2006.

4 Oborne, *The Triumph of the Political Class*.

5 Richard Seymour, 'Working-class Tories become an endangered species', *Guardian*, 17 March 2011.

6 http://news.bbc.co.uk/2/shared/bsp/hi/pdfs/BNP_uk_ manifesto.pdf.

7 The manifesto was described by the historian Nigel Copsey as 'intuitively fascist'. See Copsey, *Contemporary British Fascism*, p. 164.

8 Also in 2005, a BNP-linked 'trade union', Solidarity, was set up by Griffin's former National Front Political Soldier comrade Patrick Harrington. It had negligible impact.

9 'Most Britons actually support BNP policies', *Daily Mail*, 25 April 2006.

10 *British National Party Activists' Handbook*, 2005.

11 Personal correspondence with Ludi Simpson, professor of population studies at the University of Manchester.

12 'BNP: the Roots of its Appeal', Democratic Audit, 2006.

13 'The Far Right in London: a Challenge for Local Democracy?' Joseph Rowntree Reform Trust, 2005.

14 'Time to Improve Election Results', *Identity*, issue 99, February 2009.

15 Ibid.

16 The Gini coefficient, economists' standard measure of inequality,

which is marked on a scale of 1 to 100, stood at 25 in 1979. In the mid-1990s it was 34, and rose to 36 after 1997. From Polly Toynbee and David Walker, *The Verdict: Did Labour Change Britain?* London: Granta, 2011, p. 199.

17 Department for Work and Pensions, 'Households Below Average Income: An analysis of the income distribution 1994/95–2007/08', London 2009, p. 19.

18 Ibid., p. 137.

19 *Identity*, issue 99, February 2009.

20 Sonia Gable, 'Inept councillors had nothing to offer', 7 April 2007, hopenothate.org.uk; Source: *Searchlight*.

21 http://www.londonpatriot.org/2010/02/25/barking-and-dagenham-bnp-alternate-budget/; 'What would life be like under a BNP council? The ugly truth revealed', *Mirror*, 23 March 2010.

22 *Barking and Dagenham Sentinel*, 1 May 2010.

23 Matthew Goodwin, *New British Fascism: The Rise of the British National Party*, London: Routledge, 2011, p. 102.

24 Ibid., p. 105.

25 Ibid., p. 109.

26 D. Cutts, R. Ford and M. Goodwin, 'Anti-immigrant, politically disaffected or still racist after all? Examining the drivers of BNP support in the 2009 European Parliament elections', *European Journal of Political Research*, vol. 50, no. 3 (2011).

27 Goodwin, *New British Fascism*, p. 107.

28 A 2009 parliamentary report, for instance, indicated that journalism had become a profession taken up almost exclusively by people from middle-class backgrounds.

29 Richard Klein, 'White and working class . . . the one ethnic group the BBC has ignored', *Daily Mail*, 29 February 2008.

30 Ian Cobain, 'Exclusive: inside the secret and sinister world of the BNP', *Guardian*, 21 December 2006.

31 Goodwin, *New British Fascism*, p. 126, p. 131.

32 Vron Ware, 'Looking for Whiteness in the War on Terror', in Susan Petrilli, ed., *White Matters: Il Bianco in Questione*, Rome: Meltemi Editore, 2007, pp. 99–108.

33 *Identity*, issue 88, March 2008.

34 Matthew Taylor, 'Mother out to seize stronghold of "unforgivable" BNP', *Guardian*, 23 March 2006.

35 Ware, 'Looking for Whiteness in the War on Terror'.

36 Paul Meszaros, 'A winning formula', *Red Pepper*, August 2009.

Chapter 8. Good Fences Make Good Neighbours

1 *Daily Telegraph*, 12 June 2009.

2 *Identity*, issue 98, January 2009, p. 4.

3 http://news.bbc.co.uk/1/hi/england/8550698.stm.

4 Matthew Day and Bruno Waterfield, 'Tory MEPs "led by Pole with extremist past"', *Telegraph*, 15 July 2009.

5 In 2008, the Stoke-on-Trent Governance Commission identified a 'breakdown of conventional politics in the city'; 'widespread disillusionment'; 'fragmentation of the mainstream parties'; 'lack of ambition and purpose'; 'a feeling of hopelessness and despair'. At points, the city was run by a power-sharing coalition of Labour, Lib Dems and Conservatives.

6 Stoke Patriot blog, http://stokepatriot.blogspot.com, accessed in July 2011.

7 Interview with Sam Tarry, 10 June 2011.

8 Private information.

9 This offer, or similar offers, were reported to me by people with direct experience of BNP activity in both Stoke-on-Trent and Barking and Dagenham.

10 *Stoke Sentinel*, 19 May 2008.

11 *Stoke Sentinel*, 24 May 2008.

12 Ibid.

13 *The Times*, 29 August 2008.

14 *The Times*, 29 May 2008.

15 For example: *Stoke Sentinel*, 11 July 2007.

16 'Investigation into the response by Staffordshire Police to incidents between the Brown/Barker and Khan families on Uttoxeter Road, Stoke on Trent', IPCC References 2007/009515 and 2007/010378.

17 'Nick Griffin At Stoke Rally in Memory of Keith Brown', 20 September 2008, youtube.com.

18 BNP leaflet, circa 1998.

19 Kerry Moore, Paul Mason and Justin Lewis, 'Images of Islam in the UK: The Representation of British Muslims in the National Print News Media 2000–2008', Cardiff School of Journalism, 2008.

20 David James Smith, 'Fear and Hatred on the Streets of Luton', *The Sunday Times* 15 June 2009.

21 Interview with Nick Griffin, 24 February 2011.

22 *Searchlight*, September 2008.

Chapter 9. Political Correctness Gone Mad

1 Le Pen called his appearance on *L'Heure de vérité*, which helped soften his image and drew in a wave of new members, 'the hour that changed everything'.

2 James Macintyre, 'How the BNP came in from the cold', *New Statesman*, 22 October 2009.

3 Ibid.

4 'Five reasons why Nick Griffin should step down' by 'P Andrews' originally from BNP Ideas, the website of Andrew Brons: http://www.bnpreform2011.co.uk/?p=2478.

5 James Macintyre, 'Exclusive: Tory chair aimed for BNP votes', *Prospect*, 27 April 2011.

6 *The Times*, 20 October 2009.

7 http://martinwingfield.blogspot.com/2009/09/let-rajinder-have-honour.html.

8   Pippa Crerar, 'BNP short of candidates to take Barking and Dagenham', *Evening Standard*, 12 April 2010.

9   Gerry Gable, 'How a militant anti-abortionist took over the BNP (part 1 of a three part investigation)', *Searchlight*, November 2009, hopenothate.org.uk.

10 Figures supplied by the Barking Constituency Labour Party.

11 Anushka Asthana and Toby Helm, 'Tories caught up in new immigration storm', *Observer*, 28 February 2010.

12 George Eaton, 'Woolas pays the price', *New Statesman*, 5 November 2010.

13 *Searchlight*, June 2010.

14 Ibid.

15 Interview with Sam Tarry, 10 June 2011.

16 Private information.

17 Interview with Alby Walker, 14 April 2010.

18 Earlier in 2010, the manufacturers of Marmite had run a marketing campaign on Facebook that featured two spoof political parties – the 'Love Party' and the 'Hate Party', with the latter bearing a distinct resemblance to the BNP. Perhaps hoping to capitalize on the publicity, the BNP superimposed a photo of a Marmite jar over the first few seconds of their televised party political broadcast. Marmite's parent company, Unilever, sued. Amid recriminations over who was to blame for the stunt, the BNP's webmaster Simon Bennett resigned, switching off the BNP website as a parting shot.

19 *Searchlight*, June 2010.

20 Simon Rogers, 'General election 2010: the ultimate results map', *Guardian*, 8 May, 2010.

21 Vernon Bogdanor, 'The End of the UK', *London Review of Books*, vol. 32, no. 11, 10 June 2010.

22 Lauren Collins, 'England, their England', *The New Yorker*, 4 July 2011.

23 http://www.hopenothate.org.uk/hate-groups/edl/.

24 Lake stepped down from this role in January 2011.

25 Nick Lowles, 'Puppet master', *Searchlight*, March 2011.

26 Dipesh Gadher and Robin Henry, 'Unmasked: wealthy backers behind far-right league', *Sunday Times*, 11 December 2011, hopenothate.org.uk.

27 Lowles, 'Puppet Master'.

28 *Proud and Prejudiced*, Channel 4, 2012.

29 A survey of EDL supporters conducted via the organization's Facebook page. See Jamie Bartlett and Mark Littler, 'Inside the EDL: Populist Politics in an Internet Age', London: Demos, 2011.

30 *Proud and Prejudiced*, Channel 4, 2012.

31 Kevin Arscott, 'Winterval: the unpalatable making of a modern myth', *Guardian*, 8 November 2011.

32 Steve Hughes, 'English Defence League: we'll stand up and fight for Britain's brave heroes', *Daily Star*, 8 February 2011, dailystar.co.uk.

33 Vikram Dodd and Matthew Taylor, 'Muslims criticise Scotland Yard for telling them to engage with EDL', *Guardian*, 2 September 2011.

34 'MEP Sajjad Karim "threatened" over EDL protest by home', News Lancashire, 5 July 2011.

35 Ryan Erfani-Ghettani, 'From portrayal to reality: examining the record of the EDL', Institute of Race Relations, 8 December 2011.

36 Nick Lowles, 'Infidel leader praises the Protocols', live blog, 28 June 2011, hopenothate.org.uk.

37 Ryan Erfani-Ghettani, 'From Portrayal to Reality: Examining the Record of the EDL', Institute of Race Relations, 8 December 2011, www.irr.org.uk

38 *Searchlight*, August 2011, p. 6.

39 'EDL leader Stephen Lennon convicted of assault', News Lancashire, 29 September 2011, bbc.co.uk.

40 Private information.
41 P Andrews, 'Five Reasons Why Nick Griffin Should Step Down', BNP Reform, 18 June 2011, bnpreform2011.co.uk.
42 BNP email newsletter, August 2011.

Conclusion

1 'Thinking Behind the Numbers: Understanding Public Opinion on Immigration in Britain', Oxford: Migration Observatory, 2012.
2 Dorian Lynskey, 'Racism vs "racism": why Diane Abbott was right', live blog, January 2012, 33revolutionsperminute. wordpress.com.
3 Mark Townsend, 'Stop and search "racial profiling" by police on the increase, claims study', *Guardian*, 14 January 2012.
4 See 'More segregation or more mixing?', ethnicity.ac.uk.
5 Robert Booth, 'Rise in hate crime follows BNP council election victories', *Guardian*, 15 January 2010, guardian.co.uk.

Index